The Brothers ESPOSITO

Confrontation: Goaltender Tony Esposito and brother Phil.

The Brothers ESPOSITO

By
Phil Esposito

By
Tony Esposito

with Tim Moriarty

An Associated Features Book

HAWTHORN BOOKS, INC.
PUBLISHERS
NEW YORK

To Mother
Who sometimes played goalie

To Dad
Who stood behind us

THE BROTHERS ESPOSITO

PHOTO CREDITS

David Bier: 101
Chicago Black Hawks: 56
Esposito family collection: 10, 24, 28, 33, 54
Michigan Tech: 74
Dick Raphael: vi, 155, 169, 173
United Press International: 59, 65, 84, 112, 116, 125, 138, 151, 162, 173, 185
Wide World: 5

CONTENTS

FOREWORD

It was a blustery winter night in Boston. Phil Esposito and I had been closeted in a hotel room since mid-afternoon. Under my gentle prodding, Phil had been talking into a tape recorder for the better part of three hours. His voice was becoming hoarse, so we decided to interrupt the session for dinner.

We took the elevator to the lobby and stood on the sidewalk near the entrance to the hotel to await the arrival of Phil's business manager, Fred Sharf. While we were standing there a middle-aged man started to push his way through the revolving door. He appeared to be a commuter headed for a quick drink at the hotel bar on the way to his train.

The man did a double-take, recognized Phil and allowed the door to swing around and deposit him back on the street. He walked up to Phil, shook his hand and said, "You're having a great season, young fellow. Keep it up and good luck." Phil thanked the man, watched him reenter the hotel and said, "It's always nice to be recognized."

Two weeks later, I was in a hotel in Chicago. This time my companion was Tony Esposito. We had just finished a taping session and were riding down in the elevator. A matronly woman tugged at Tony's arm and said, "I know who you are and I think you're a wonderful goaltender. God love you."

Tony expressed his appreciation, then turned to me and said, "It's always nice to be recognized."

All sorts of people—not only hockey fans—have come to recognize the Esposito brothers. Phil and Tony have reached the point where they are regarded as the most exciting, refreshing brother act in ice hockey.

Their story is a unique one, starting in the days when they were boys in Sault Ste. Marie, Ontario. The brothers are the sons of second-generation Italian-Canadian parents who taught them the basic values of being honest, sincere and fair-minded.

These characteristics and their common goals on ice are where the brotherly similarity ends. Phil, 14 months older than Tony, is one of hockey's most engaging characters. He is witty, gregarious and, though lacking in academic degrees, a man of insight with native intelligence.

Tony, a college graduate, lacks Phil's *savoir faire*. He broods more after a defeat, is hard to know and generally a person of few words. Yet he can be light-hearted and fun-loving when he forgets his last game and relaxes with friends.

Physically, the brothers bear a slight facial resemblance. They are dark-haired, dark-visaged and beetle-browed. Phil is taller, packing two hundred ten pounds on his six-foot, one-inch frame. Tony, two inches shorter, weighs a stocky one hundred eighty-five.

Though intense rivals on the ice, a strong bond exists between them. It is the bond of brotherly love. For as youngsters they shared the same dream—to become stars in the National Hockey League.

They've gone their separate ways and have come to wear different uniforms—Phil in Boston, Tony in Chicago. They respect each other as professionals. And they don't pull their punches when talking about other players, their coaches, or each other.

A nationwide television audience can attest to Phil's candor on a night in May, 1971, when Tony erred in giving up a critical goal to the Montreal Canadiens and Phil, as TV analyst, said without hesitation, "Well, Tony blew that one."

That's the only way Phil would ever call it. Reverse the situation, and Tony would have said, "Well, Phil blew that one."

These are the Brothers Esposito.

TIM MORIARTY
Rockville Centre, N.Y.

CHAPTER 1

BROTHER AGAINST BROTHER

Phil and Tony Esposito followed different routes to the National Hockey League and it wasn't until the night of December 5, 1968, that their paths finally crossed on the frozen surface of Boston Garden. For the first time since their street hockey days back in Sault Ste. Marie, they found themselves on opposing teams. It was one of the most historic moments in the annals of pro hockey. And even though he was the veteran, Phil approached the game with some apprehension.

I think I was more nervous than Tony that night. In fact, it was probably the most frightful game of my entire hockey career. I had been a pro since 1962 and was then in my sixth season in the NHL. I was an established player getting ready to shoot pucks at my own brother, who had been in the league only one week.

When I had heard Tony had been called up by the Canadiens from Houston I was excited for him and glad. Now, suddenly, here he was in Boston and I was concerned about the game and his future.

Tony telephoned me the afternoon of the game. He told me about his debut with the Canadiens in Oakland six nights earlier when he had relieved Rogie Vachon in the second period and the Canadiens lost, 5–4.

"That was only one game, your first game, so don't let it bug you," I said. "You'll get other chances to show 'em what you can do."

"Right," Tony said. "Like tonight. Claude Ruel is going to give me my first start against you guys."

I gulped a couple of times because this was the first hint I had that Ruel was about to give Tony his second chance.

"Well, good luck, Tony," I said. "And don't be too tough on the star of the family." He laughed. It was a nervous laugh.

When I hung up the phone, I was seized by a strange feeling. Would this be the start or finish of Tony's career? Would I be the cause of him being sent down and never making it to the NHL again?

You need the breaks to make the NHL and more breaks to last in the league. This is especially true with goalies. I wanted to see Tony get the breaks he was entitled to. I also knew I had eighteen other players depending on me. I couldn't let them down.

Those thoughts kept rushing through my mind as I drove to Boston Garden that night. When I got there, I didn't attempt to see Tony. "Better not fraternize with the enemy," I told myself.

I walked into the Bruins' dressing room and Danny Canney, one of our trainers, whispered to me he had heard Tony would be playing tonight. Then, while getting into my uniform, Harry Sinden walked over to me and in a voice loud enough for all the players to hear, said, "Your brother is starting against us."

That's when the guys started bugging me a little. It was mostly good-natured kidding. Fred Stanfield hollered across the room at me. "You going to try tonight, Phil, or just fool around because it's your brother in the other net?"

Derek Sanderson said, "Just shoot the damn puck at the Wop. He can't stop anything."

By the time we went out on the ice I was really uptight. Then the fans got on me during the warmup. They saw Tony handling practice shots in the Montreal net and figured he would start.

One fan hollered, "You going to throw the game, Phil?" That really burned me up. There was no way I was going to do that. I was ready to play my best and I knew Tony would play his best.

When the National Anthem was played before the start of the game, I said a little prayer. I asked God first to look over my mother. She was back home with my dad. I knew she hadn't been feeling well and I didn't want this game to affect her condition. I also prayed that Tony would play well and I would play well and that neither one of us would cause our teams or our family any embarrassment.

Then I looked across the ice at Tony. He was rocking back and forth in front of the Montreal net. I wondered if he was more nervous than I was.

Tony was so jittery leading up to that game that even now he claims it is difficult for him to recreate all the incidents surrounding his first NHL start.

I must have been in a real fog because I can't remember phoning Phil that afternoon and telling him I was going to start. But if he claims I called, accept his word for it. He wouldn't lie.

There were two reasons why Claude Ruel chose me to play against the Bruins that night. Two days earlier, during a routine practice in Montreal, Rogie Vachon raised his stick hand to ward off a shot by Jacques Lemaire. The shot broke a bone in Vachon's right hand. Now the Canadiens had two goalies on the sidelines — Vachon and Gump Worsley.

The night following Vachon's injury, the Canadiens played the Rangers at Montreal. Ruel apparently wasn't willing to trust me with that assignment, so he called up Ernie Wakely from Cleveland. Wakely was shaky as hell. He had been kicking around in the Montreal farm system for eight years and this was his first NHL game. He gave up a couple of bad goals and the Rangers won, 4–2.

Wakely and I both made the trip to Boston. The Canadiens now were in a real bind. Who would Ruel start against the Bruins? A shaky old farmhand like Wakely or a shaky young farmhand like Tony Esposito. Ruel chose me.

If Phil claims he was nervous before that game, imagine how I felt? Especially when Ruel gave me the assignment. He said, "I'm giving you another chance. I know the Bruins are tough, but give it your best, one hundred per cent, you know, and try to be relaxed."

Good old Claude. How the hell could I relax knowing I was about to face the Bruins and my own brother, who was then tearing the league apart?

Sitting in the visiting team's dressing room at Boston Garden, trying to get into my pads, I knew Phil was just down the corridor in the Boston locker room. I figured some of his guys were needling him about playing against his brother.

None of the Montreal players gave me the business. They could see I was nervous and, happily, they left me alone with my thoughts. I wondered if this would be a make-or-break game for me. And, naturally, I wondered how I would react if Phil skated in on me and fired one of those wicked shots of his.

It didn't take Phil long to test me. With about eight minutes gone in the first period, he took a pass from Ted Green and banged his shot off a post and into the net. It was a lucky shot.

Phil's version of that first goal differs slightly.

How could Tony call it lucky? It was a work of art. Green passed to me in front of Larry Hillman, who was then playing defense for Montreal. I swept around Hillman and tried to shoot the puck between Tony's right pad and the post. The puck hit the post, bounced across, hit the other post and went in.

I remember Tony getting the puck out of the net and shooting it. For a second, I thought he was aiming at me. He was teed off, the same way he used to get when I'd beat him in our pick-up games as kids. But this time he was just shooting the puck down the ice so he would have a little more time to recover from my goal.

Tony seemed to settle down after Montreal tied the score on a second-period goal by Bobby Rousseau. He was making some good saves and I thought at the time it would be perfect if the game ended in a tie.

The Boston fans must have been having the same thoughts. They seemed to be rooting for the both of us. They knew how much this game meant to Tony and his future. Whenever he'd make a stop, they would cheer him. And every time I got the puck they would cheer me.

The crowd stopped cheering Tony, though, when Yvan Cournoyer beat Gerry Cheevers to put Montreal ahead, 2–1, early in the final period. Now they were just rooting for me.

With about eleven minutes left to play, I skated onto the ice with my linemates, Ken Hodge and Ron Murphy. I could hear the

Phil scores against Tony in their first NHL encounter.

fans yelling, "Go get 'em, Phil . . . Beat your brother, Phil . . . Don't let the kid beat you." That really psyched me up.

I glanced at Tony standing in front of the Montreal net and mumbled to myself, "Better be on your toes, Tony. Here comes your big brother."

Bobby Orr trapped a loose puck near center ice and gave me a perfect lead pass. As I got across the blueline, I let it rip. I was using a big, curved stick then that made the puck do funny things. It started to rise and then dipped about a foot, maybe two feet, and caught a corner of the net.

I had beaten Tony again, mainly because I don't think he expected me to shoot from such a distance. He was surprised.

According to Tony, it was another lucky shot.

I wasn't surprised by Phil's second goal — just aggravated. It was partially screened, but it's a shot I should have stopped. On some screen shots the goalie never has a chance. It will come flying between a half dozen bodies or a dozen legs and wind up in the cage without the goalie getting a glimpse of it.

Phil's shot came from far out — maybe fifty feet. I caught sight of it as it flew between somebody's legs, grabbed for it and missed. That's what annoyed me. Even though it dropped a little like a sinker or a knuckleball, I should have gotten a glove on it.

It tied the score at 2–2 and that's the way the game ended. I was happy about that because any time you can tie in Boston, well, you've done your job, believe me.

There were times in that game, though, that I was fortunate. The Bruins had me in real trouble on several occasions but they made the wrong move and I got off the hook. Phil didn't utter a word to me after either of his goals. But once, after I stopped one of the Bruins — I think it was Ken Hodge — he skated by me, covered his mouth with a glove and said, "Nice save, Bomby." That's the nickname Phil had given me when we were kids.

I appreciated the brotherly encouragement. But I didn't appreciate the fact he had beaten me twice, and I told him so after the game. We talked for maybe five minutes before I rushed for the team bus which was taking us to the airport.

"You were lucky on the first goal and lucky on the second goal," I said.

Phil just laughed. He said, "What the hell, Tony, I'm just a lucky guy."

He then told me that the Boston goalies, Cheevers and Ed Johnston, had come to him after the game and said they liked my style.

"Gerry and Ed both said you're going to be a good one," Phil said. "They said you're going to make this league and be around for a long time."

Now, I really felt happy. In my happiness I was almost ready to forgive Phil for scoring the only two goals off me in my first NHL start.

Phil insisted on adding a postscript to the game.
It concerns Tony's wife, Marilyn.

I got a phone call that night from Marilyn in Houston. She hadn't been able to reach Tony after the game and Tony, rushing to catch the Canadiens' flight back to Montreal, was unable to call her.

When I picked up the phone, Marilyn said, "Well?" I said, "Well, what?" I was teasing her and she didn't like it.

"You know why I'm calling, Phil. What happened tonight? What was the final score?"

"It was a tie, 2–2," I said. "Tony played great."

"Good," she said. "Did you get a goal?"

"Yeah, Marilyn, I got the first one."

"Who got the second one?"

"I got that one, too."

"Phil," she screamed over the phone, "you're a dirty dog."

CHAPTER 2

BROKEN WINDOWS

The formative years of the Espositos were not unlike those of most young boys growing up in Sault Ste. Marie, a steel mill town carved out of the wilderness of Western Ontario. The Soo, as it is known to the natives, lies directly across the St. Mary's River from its twin city of Sault Ste. Marie, Michigan. Young boys in the Soo learn to skate not long after they learn to walk. In Phil Esposito's case, his debut on skates was slightly delayed.

Considering my lanky frame, this might be difficult for some people to understand now, but I was a chubby rascal as a baby. My parents tell me I weighed in at eleven pounds at my birth on February 20, 1942. Tony was born fourteen months later, on April 23, 1943, and weighed nine pounds. He learned to walk first — maybe because he wasn't carrying as much weight around as I.

Sitting around my father's house recently, he was kidding me about the fact that it took me so long to stand up on my own two feet.

"Geez," he said, "You were maybe twenty-five or twenty-six months old before you learned to walk. I remember taking you and Tony with me to visit friends. I'd be carrying you, and Tony would walk alongside. People would come up to me and say, 'Hey, Pat, how come Phil isn't walking yet? What is he lazy, or something?' And I'd have to make excuses for you and tell the people you were just tired."

Naturally, I don't remember my father carrying me in his arms at that age, but I must have got my legs to support me by the time I was three because it wasn't long after that I started skating.

When I was between three and four years old, my dad built a rink for me and Tony in the backyard of our first house on Alexandra Street in the West End of the Soo. We had apple trees in the backyard and we used two of these to form a sort of goal as they were spaced about four or five feet apart.

Tony and I had our first pickup games behind the house. We used to play with our cousin, Danny DiPietro, who was a real baby then, and two other close friends, Ross Hryharchuk and Clem Giovannatti.

There was a big outdoor rink at our school, the King Edward School, a block away and we would skate there, too. And when it became icy and slippery and the roads were frozen we would put on our skates and play in the street in front of our house.

Tony and I would play by ourselves or we'd get two other guys and practice shooting. One guy would be the goaltender and the others would shoot and the guy with the fewest goals would take over in goal. Tony won't like me saying this, but he always lost. I guess you could say that's how he wound up as a goalie.

I remember my first pair of skates had two blades. They were double runners, actually, the kind you tie to your shoes or boots with a leather strap. They weren't new, either. Probably hand-me-downs from relatives.

The year after I started with the double runners, my dad bought me my first pair of hockey skates. They were used tubular skates and I got them as a Christmas present. I think we went to some bargain basement store in the Soo and picked them up there.

Tony was more fortunate — he didn't have to launch his career on double runners.

I can't remember Phil's first skates, but I know my first pair were single blades. I was about five years old when I got them. They were used baby skates and not tempered steel like you find in the more expensive ones. I think they were given to me by one of my cousins.

Phil (front row center) and Tony (glasses) at King Edward School.

Phil and I would go to the rink at the school and when I laced them on I really thought they were something. I don't remember ever having them sharpened so I don't know how I ever learned to skate with them. But they did fit okay.

Again, Phil was less fortunate. His first hockey skates didn't fit properly.

They were too damn big, believe me. I used two or three pair of woolen socks, the dark blue or gray ones that workmen wear, to fill up the boots so they wouldn't be too loose. Looking back now I can remember when I was ten or eleven and I was using size eleven skates. I now use size ten, so you can figure it out. My early skates were hardly ideal.

But the big thing was that Tony and I loved to skate and play hockey. We played a game called "Pump, Pump, Pullaway." A lot of the dekes (fakes) and moves I use now could be attributed to what I learned in this game. And I'm sure it helped Tony's reflexes, too.

Here's how the game was played: One guy would stand in the middle of the rink and maybe ten or eleven of us would stand at one end. The one in the center would holler, "Pump, pump, pullaway," and the rest of us would head down ice and try to get to the snowbank at the other end without being tagged.

The first guy tagged would join the one in the middle in trying to tag the others. It would continue that way, with each guy caught joining the group in the center. The object, of course, was to avoid being tagged.

Very often I would be the last guy caught. I was pretty shifty even then. I'd skate backwards or slow down and then look for a good opening. Sometimes I'd make it through the whole gang without being touched.

Tony's fondest memories of those early days were the pickup hockey games after classes at the King Edward elementary school.

Phil and I would rush home from school, do a little homework and then have pickup games either in the street or at the school rink. The games would last for hours and we'd even play at night under the street lights.

At dinner time, my father would whistle for us and we'd come home and sit at the table with our skates on. My mother would spread newspapers so we wouldn't ruin the floor. Then, fifteen minutes later, after gulping down our food, we'd be back playing on the street or the rink.

We lived across the street from our church, Blessed Sacrament. The pastor was Msgr. O'Leary. He was a nice enough man, but he used to get tired of our games in the street — hockey in the winter and softball in the summer. I guess we made a lot of noise. We also broke a few windows in the Monsignor's garage.

There was always hell to pay when we broke one of those windows. The Monsignor would come rushing out of the rectory, screaming at us. And, you know, for a priest he used pretty strong language.

We broke other windows around the neighborhood and sometimes we'd even get blamed for windows we didn't break. I remember once this man came to our house and claimed my father owed him money for windows we supposedly broke at his place. My father called me and Phil into the house for a confrontation with the man.

"Did you break any windows at this man's house?" he asked. "And don't give me any baloney. I want the truth."

Phil and I were shaking in our boots.

"I didn't do anything," Phil said.

"Me, either," I said.

My father, who is a big man of about two hundred fifty pounds, then turned on the man.

"My boys have never lied to me and I don't think they're lying now," he said. "So you better get the hell out of my house before I throw you out."

The man took off like a giant bird. And, you know, to this day I can't ever remember lying to my father. He was a man who demanded respect and he got it from me and Phil.

In many other ways, though, my father has always been easy going. He had it tough growing up, but he took good care of us.

His own father settled in the Soo after arriving in Canada from Naples, Italy, around 1900 and worked in the mills for fifty years.

There were seven children in dad's family. Dad quit grade school to go to work and sailed on ore carriers on the Great Lakes when he was fifteen. He later worked as a common laborer for thirty-three cents an hour, then got a job as a welder for forty-two cents an hour with Algoma Contractors, a trucking company dealing in scrap and slag recovery. The company was originally owned by my grandfather, and following his death my uncles Nick and Danny DiPietro took over. They later sold it to Ogden Metals.

It was while dad was still learning the welding trade that he married my mother — her maiden name was Frances DiPietro — in 1941. He built the first house on Alexandra Street for three thousand dollars and had it completely paid for in six years. Then the money started to roll in for us.

My father progressed from welder to foreman to general foreman and now is general superintendent at Algoma, where he earns a good salary. He's a real success story and a self-made man and, naturally, we're very proud of him.

People often ask me if Phil and I fought as kids and how we were punished. Well, we argued a lot and we'd get into fist fights, sometimes with each other and sometimes with other guys. But dad never was too tough on us. He'd spank us once in a while, but mostly he'd just try to scare us.

Speak for yourself, Tony. Your brother remem-
bers plenty of arguments and fights which produced
more than love taps from your father.

You bet we fought, but no more than most brothers. Tony and I would squabble mostly over clothes and hockey equipment. He'd say, "That's my hockey stick." And I'd say, "No, that's my hockey stick." Crazy arguments like that. So we'd fight a lot in the house and on the street or at the rink.

I guess I used to bug him a lot. Like when he'd be sleeping late in the morning, I'd drive him nuts by hitting him over the head with a pillow.

There was this one morning when I hit Tony with a pillow

and got him real sore. We were both in T-shirts and he reached out and scratched me across the back with his fingernails. Now Tony had real sharp fingernails because he didn't bite them like some kids. He cut me across the back pretty good, drawing blood.

I didn't want to complain to my folks because I figured he'd get a damn good licking and maybe I'd get it, too, so I went across the street to my aunt's house and she took care of me.

I'll tell you this, too: I still have scars on my back from Tony's fingernails.

So we fought a lot as kids, but no one could say my brother was a jerk to my face or make fun of him in any way or else I'd take on the guy. And I'm sure Tony felt the same way about me.

I remember some other great fights — the Esposito brothers against the Longarini brothers, Carlo and John. They'll probably laugh at the memory themselves. We used to really go at it. And then we'd pair off against other kids. I don't know if it was by design or it just happened. Sometimes we won, sometimes we lost.

And when it came to punishing us, my father didn't spare the rod. Oh, he never used a switch or stick on us, you understand, and he never denied us meals for punishment. He'd just give us a good kick in the ass, real hard, too, because he's a big man and a strong bugger.

One of the best kicks I ever got was when Tony and I were real young. He was probably seven and I was eight. You know how kids always try smoking? Well, we tried it in the basement of our house and set it on fire.

My dad had been painting and fixing up the rec room, so we sat down there one day and started rolling our own cigarettes and smoking them. There was a lot of rags and paper around and we got careless with the matches and a fire started.

I yelled to my father upstairs, "Hey, dad, the place is on fire." He came bouncing down the stairs, got us out of there, then stamped out the burning paper and rags. He got burned, not severely, but all the hair on his chest and some on his head got singed.

Geez, we got some good kicks from him that day.

CHAPTER III

MOTHER PLAYS GOALIE

As teenagers, the Espositos had interests other than hockey. They developed a fondness for girls, which got them into occasional trouble, and a fondness for borrowing cars without permission, which also got them into trouble. Phil, as the older brother, generally wound up accepting the blame — and the consequences — for these juvenile pranks.

I was either fourteen or fifteen when Tony and I stole our first car. Actually, Tony was just a spectator. I stole it, or maybe I should say I borrowed it, because it belonged to my dad. At any rate, I didn't ask his permission. How could I? I didn't have a license.

So while my mother and father were out on this particular day, I took the car — it was a Monarch, I think — and we drove off with Tony in the front seat next to me and my sister Terry, who was then only a baby, in the back seat.

Hey, we really had a ball. We drove down Queen Street, that's the main drag in the Soo, and we picked up this girl and headed for one of the city's parks. I didn't know it at the time, but my folks spotted us and beat us back to the house.

When I pulled into the driveway, my father was waiting for me. Tony ran into the house with my sister. I took off down the street with my father chasing me.

He chased me around the block and — this is no lie — every time he got close to me he'd kick me in the rear end. And when he'd kick me I'd go up about three feet in the air. I was yelping and he was hollering and, believe me, it was some scene.

"Hey, dad, that hurts," I kept saying with each kick.

15

"Oh, yeah," he said. "Well, by God, I want it to hurt."

So I kept running like hell until I circled the block and got home. When I got there, Tony was already in bed, sleeping. I think he got a slap in the head, but I took all the blame. It was my fault because I had talked him into it.

I guess I didn't learn much from that thrashing because when I was sixteen I took off with my father's car again. I had a learner's permit at the time, but I wasn't supposed to be out alone.

This time I went through a traffic light and bumped into a parked car and left without reporting it. They got me, though. The owner of the parked car came to the house and said he was ready to press charges against me. Oh, oh! I was scared as hell.

My dad? Boy, he was mad again. He paid the guy off — one hundred bucks plus damage costs to the car. Then he gave me another real licking.

The damndest thing about all this trouble I was getting into was that it happened after we had moved from Alexandra Street in the West End of the Soo to Shannon Road in a more respectable neighborhood in the East End. I remember my dad explaining at the time why we were moving.

"You boys are staying out too late at night," he said, "and I'm having a little trouble keeping you in line."

The West End then probably would have been classified as lower middle class. It was strictly an Italian district, and it was kind of rough. I don't want to make it sound as rough as the neighborhood Derek Sanderson said he grew up in in Niagara Falls, but it was rough.

It had a lot of people living there who worked hard for their money in the steel plants. They worked hard and they lived hard. They were tough. The environment itself, though, wasn't that bad. Everybody was friendly and knew everybody else in the neighborhood.

And we had some pretty good kids in and around our block. Bennie Greco was one of them. He was one of the best of the young players I had ever seen. Tough but good. I don't know what happened to that poor kid, whether he wound up in a bad situation or not, but he was a damn good hockey player.

There was another young kid we grew up with back there in the West End who hanged himself. That really shook up the neighborhood. But, all told, it wasn't that bad. You can ask Tony.

Tony's version of his life and times in the West End differs only slightly from Phil's.

I really enjoyed living there — our first house on Alexandra Street was great and so were the kids we played with. We had our own little gang. There was Phil and I, Danny Vresk and Gino Cavicchiolo. We were like Musketeers — four Musketeers.

We go into a little trouble once in a while. But there were no major incidents, just minor violations like disturbing the peace. We did get nailed by the police for that a couple of times. And staying out late at night and playing around in the back alleys.

Our major interest, though, was playing hockey. There were some winter mornings when I'd climb out of bed when it was still dark outside and head for the outdoor rink at Central Park about two and a half blocks from our house on Alexandra Street.

It would be maybe ten below zero and there would be a lot of snow on the ground, but I didn't seem to mind it. I'd pile my goalie pads and other equipment on a sled — I was too young to carry that stuff in my arms — and pull the sled down the street.

On the way to the rink I'd stop at the house of John Lanoce, whom we called "Clipper." He was a little older and was one of my first coaches. He didn't always appreciate my waking him so early on cold mornings.

Clipper would come to the window of his bedroom and yell, "What the hell do you want, Tony?"

"I'm going down to the rink to practice. Come on and join me."

"Go back to bed where you belong," he'd answer and slam the window in my face.

So I'd continue on to the rink alone, but Clipper would join me later and so would Phil and we'd play and play and play until we were exhausted.

Clipper is forever reminding me of a game we played at the Central Park rink when Phil and I were quite young. We were teammates on this team coached by Clipper. The score was tied in the third period when a guy on the other team fired a shot from center ice.

I wore glasses then but I took them off for this particular game. I never saw the shot. It was a high shot and in those days anybody who shot high was a hero. This guy wound up the hero because I fanned on it and Phil really tore into me.

"You can't see a damn thing," Phil yelled. "You're blind."

Then Clipper tore into Phil.

"You've got some nerve picking on Tony," he said. "Who the hell is running this club, anyway? I'm the boss, not you, so keep your damn mouth shut."

My parents used to come to those early games and they gave it to Phil, too, for picking on me.

Incidentally, I don't know how my folks survived those games in such cold weather. We didn't mind it because just the excitement of the games helped us forget the cold. But they would stand around on the snowbanks piled high along the sideboards and the temperature would be below zero.

At the end of the games, we would rush home and dad would take off our boots and rub the numbness out of our toes before putting us to bed.

That was one of the reasons we liked living in the West End: It was so close to the rink. And we got to know a few girls there, too. But let my brother handle this.

Phil isn't bashful about discussing the opposite sex.

Ah, girls. We used to chase them a lot when we were kids. Tony and I once trapped this girl near our school. I was about eleven years old and Tony was ten. We tried to kiss her and fool around, but we didn't get very far because we really didn't know what we were doing or how to do it. Then a man came out of a nearby house and chased us. We didn't fool around like that for a while because the whole incident scared us.

Another time my dad caught us with a girl in the shack that we used as a clubhouse for our gang. We were fourteen or fifteen at the time. Like a lot of kids who grew up in the early fifties, we had formed a sort of motorcycle gang. But we had no motorcycles, just black leather jackets with the skull and crossbones, that type of jazz.

So the whole gang was in the shack with this girl. She was about our age and we were trying to make out with her as all kids do in their early teens. We were using one of the guys as a lookout, but he must have fallen asleep because he never saw my father approaching the shack.

Dad walked in, let loose with a yell and everybody took off. My cousin, Danny DiPietro, and I got caught with the girl. Danny dashed out so fast he cut his head on a nail and I got such a whipping, well, I'll never forget it.

It wasn't long after that incident we moved to a wonderful ranch bungalow on Shannon Road. This house had everything — an inter-com system, stereo and hi-fi, and large rooms, including a recreation room that must have measured thirty by forty feet.

We used to hold some great practice sessions in that rec room. Instead of using a puck, we'd get an old sock, a big one, and roll it up and tie it with a ribbon. Then Tony and I would take turns shooting with the sock, which would slide very easily across the floor.

Most of the time, Tony was the goaltender. But I remember my mother coming downstairs to check on us and we'd put her in goal. She'd get down on her hands and knees and we'd shoot at her. After beating her a couple of times, she would say, "Okay, boys, that's enough. You're taking advantage of your poor mother." Then she would return to her kitchen and prepare our next meal.

My mother couldn't play goal too well, but she was a great cook. One meal I loved then, which I haven't had since I was a kid, was a special dish consisting of smelts and dandelion greens. We'd have that with fresh Italian bread from the bakery. Man, that was a feast. Tony, though, didn't like the greens. He said they tickled his throat.

There was nothing wrong with his mother's other special Italian dishes, according to Tony.

We used to have a lot of spaghetti and meatballs, of course. And home-made macaroni. My dad insisted on that. He used to come home from work between four-thirty and five o'clock in the afternoon and we would sit right down to eat.

On Fridays, before we Catholics were allowed to eat meat, we'd have ravioli with ricotta cheese. And a lot of soup, like pasta fagioli, and salads. On other days there was always a lot of meat on the table — chops and steaks, mostly round steak which Phil and I love to this day.

Our favorite snack between meals was popcorn. Phil could eat it by the bushel. We'd sit in front of the radio or the television set on Saturday nights, eating popcorn, drinking soda and tuned in to the hockey games from Toronto and Montreal.

I used to root for the Canadiens then and Phil would root for Detroit. I liked Rocket Richard. First of all, he was a fighter. He was also a great goal scorer and always seemed to get the big goals. Phil liked Gordie Howe.

After watching those TV games we'd lie in bed and talk about our heroes and what it would be like to play in the National Hockey League.

Phil would say, "How would you like to try stopping Gordie Howe some day?"

And I'd say, "Yeah, it would be great. And how would you like to try shooting against Terry Sawchuk or Jacques Plante?"

Then we'd fall asleep and dream about playing in the NHL. But, you know, they were just dreams then. I never thought I'd actually make it. In fact, up to maybe four years ago I didn't think I'd get there. Phil had more confidence than I did in that respect.

According to Phil, he never lacked confidence. It was his inability to avoid trouble as a teenager that hampered him.

In public school, I was a real bad guy. Especially with the girls. I used to pull their bras in the back and snap them. It was the same thing in high school. I was a big wheel, or thought I was, and tried to act the part. I failed to pass ninth grade and that's how Tony, who had been a year behind, caught up with me.

The reason I failed was simple: I was a real jerk. I actually liked going to school and all that went with it, but I didn't care for homework. I hated it. I couldn't do it. And I fooled around constantly.

When we moved to the East End, my father was making good dough. But even though we had all that money and were living in a different and better neighborhood, I still faced a lot of problems growing up. And I did a lot of crazy things.

Tony and I were so active, which is the way kids should be, I suppose. We played street hockey and baseball and football and drove our neighbors nuts on Shannon Road. We broke a lot of windows and some of the neighbors would yell at us and we'd yell back at them.

And then there were the girls. There weren't as many in the East End as the West End, but I got to know those worth knowing. There was one girl who lived across the street from us. Her name was Jane. I used to dig her pretty good. We went out a couple of times. Other times I used to sneak into her house and sit on the couch with her and we'd neck like crazy.

But my interest in girls and my lack of interest in school didn't help me solve the other problems of growing up back there in the Soo.

CHAPTER IV

"I'M NOT A QUITTER"

Phil didn't simply pick up a hockey stick in his first organized game and emerge as a scoring champion; Tony didn't become an All-Star goalie overnight.

The Espositos became so discouraged with their lack of progress during their amateur days they even quit playing hockey for brief periods. Phil remembers failing to earn a berth on a bantam team — the equivalent of a Little League baseball team.

Tony and I first started playing together on a minor bantam team in the Soo. The players ranged in age from ten to twelve. Like Little League baseball, you reported for tryouts with all the kids in your age bracket in the entire city. This was before the city hockey leagues were divided into zones. You can imagine the competition — and the confusion.

I can't even guess how many kids showed up on the day I had my first tryout, but there were hundreds. And everything rested on that first tryout. If you didn't make it you were dead. You didn't get a second chance.

They had us kids go through the usual tests like skating, shooting, and puck-handling. I was pretty lanky for my age and a little awkward, but I thought I did well in the tryout. And when one guy came to me and said, "Phil, you're going to make it," I felt pretty good.

They started calling out the names of those who had passed the test — first one group was called and then another. I waited and waited for my name to be called. And while I waited, I prayed. But my name wasn't called.

What a blow that was! I went home crying my eyes out. How I cried! My parents tried to console me, but it was no use. I was the most disappointed kid in the Soo.

I didn't play hockey at all that year. I just fooled around, moaning a lot and cursing the entire world.

The following year I finally got my big chance when the bantam league was divided into zones. Now, instead of competing against kids from the entire city, I tried out with those from our own neighborhood in the West End. We formed what was known as Zone Seven.

I couldn't control my joy when I made the Zone Seven team. Now I was ready to show the world how good I was. The disappointment and the tears of the past season were forgotten.

It was a helluva team, too. Tony was our goalie and most of our other friends and schoolmates were on the team. Our coach was John (Clipper) Lanoce, a good friend and neighbor who spent a lot of time teaching us fundamentals. He also was kept busy breaking up arguments between me and Tony.

In those days, Tony wore glasses while playing goal. The glasses would fog up on him during a game and when he'd miss a shot I'd get on him pretty good. I have to admit now I wasn't the kindest guy in the world in the way I treated him.

There were other times when Tony teed me off with his attitude. I don't think at that period of our lives that we shared the same dreams. Oh, I know Tony liked hockey and he played hard, but I was obsessed with the idea of one day playing in the National Hockey League. It wasn't that much of an obsession with him.

Even the teachers at school became aware of my dreams. One in particular — I can't remember her name — used to question me about my plans.

"What do you want to be when you grow up?" she would ask.

"That's easy," I would answer. "I want to be a pro hockey player."

"Oh, that would be nice as a hobby," she would say, "but what profession are you interested in?"

That poor teacher just wouldn't believe me, or maybe she didn't

Bespectacled Tony (front row) with the Soo Black Hawks.

understand me. I often wonder now if she's still around and asking the same questions and shaking her head and saying, "Well, that would be nice as a hobby."

In those bantam team days, Tony and I would get up at four or five in the morning and head for the Memorial Gardens. Many of our games started at six so we didn't want to be late.

The Gardens is the principal indoor rink in the Soo. It's a good-sized building, clean and neat. It once served as the home rink of the Soo Thunderbirds in the old Eastern Professional Hockey League. It's now used mainly by the Soo Greyhounds of the Northern Ontario Hockey Association, a Junior A team sponsored by my dad and several friends.

The Esposito brothers, by the way, weren't the only NHL players to get their start in the Memorial Gardens. The Maki brothers, Wayne and Chico, played their first organized games there. So did Matt Ravlich, Lou Nanne, Gene Ubriaco, and Jerry Korab.

After our games at the Gardens, Tony and I would walk home together, have a bite to eat, and then go out and get in more practice. There were days, though, when Tony would beg off and this used to tee me off.

I'd say, "Hey, Tony, let's go out and play, do a little shooting and skating."

He'd shrug his shoulders and say, "Aw, I'm tired. I don't want to play now. Let's just hang around the house."

Then I'd get real mad and call him lazy and he'd call me a few harsh names. But we'd later apologize and soon be back playing street hockey or skating and fooling around at the rink.

Tony and I continued to play together in the bantams until I was fourteen and got a chance to move up to a midget league team managed by Angelo Bumbacco, a close friend of my dad's. I suffered another major disappointment that year.

After taking only two shifts on the ice under Angelo's watchful eyes, he cut me. "You just can't skate well enough for this league yet, Phil," he told me. "Maybe you're growing too fast. But whatever it is, you're still too awkward."

So I went back to the bantams and got my revenge on Angelo

at the end of the season when Tony and I helped beat one of his teams.

The following year, after I had turned fifteen, I made the jump to the midgets, leaving Tony behind me. We didn't play on the same team again until three years later — my last year in the juvenile ranks.

Tony Esposito can also remember his share of
heartbreaks in the Soo amateur ranks.

I didn't encounter the disappointments that Phil did in the bantams; mine came later. I was only nine when I broke into the minor bantams and found myself playing with ten- and eleven-year-old kids. I considered myself very fortunate that the people in charge thought I was good enough to play with the older guys.

One of the first championship teams I played on was the Sportsmen A.C., a bantam team coached by Ron Corbett. In 1957, when I was approaching my fourteenth birthday, our major bantam team, coached by Clipper Lanoce, beat North Bay for the Northern Ontario championship. That was a great thrill.

Two years later, I got another thrill when our midget league team, the Soo Black Hawks, won the All-Ontario championship and I was named the team's Most Valuable Player.

Up to that point in my amateur career, I was viewing the world through rose-colored glasses. Or so it seemed. Actually, I had discarded my own horn-rimmed glasses in favor of contact lenses by the time I graduated into the Juvenile ranks and joined Phil on the Soo Contractors for the 1959-60 season.

I was then sixteen years old. Phil was seventeen and had been a member of the Contractors for two years and helped them to two Northern Ontario Juvenile "A" titles. The regular goalie was Pat Nardini, but shortly after I joined the Contractors we started sharing the job. We split the assignment through most of the regular season.

Then came the playoffs and the first real kick in the pants of my career. Abbie Naccarato, our coach, decided to go with Nardini as his playoff goalie. Looking back on it now, Abbie was probably right. Nardini was more experienced, this was his last season in juvenile hockey and I was a newcomer.

Still, I had finished the season with a better average than Nardini and figured I deserved to start at least one game. So I sat on the bench and fumed. And every chance I got I bitched a little to our coach.

After one game I went to Abbie and said, "How about using me?" He was a stern man who didn't appreciate me bugging him that way. "I'm using Nardini because he's got more experience than you," he said. "You might think I'm wrong, but I think I'm right. And I'm the boss."

I couldn't resist getting in the last word.

"Well, one day we'll see who was right," I said. "We'll see who goes farther in this game . . . me or Nardini."

It was a juvenile remark made by a kid playing on a juvenile team. I remembered that incident, though, when I made the grade in the National Hockey League.

What happened to Pat Nardini? He eventually lost interest in hockey and wound up a school teacher. He's a fine fellow and I never held anything against him. I was just so anxious to get into those playoffs.

Anyway, the Contractors, with Nardini in goal and me sitting and stewing on the bench, went on to win the All-Ontario championship that year. It was truly a great team.

Phil was then coming into his own and scoring goals by the bushel. He centered a line that had Jim Sanko at right wing and Richard Lackowich at left wing.

That line must have been one of the greatest amateur lines of all time. In one playoff game against Garson, Phil scored four goals and four assists, Lackowich had three goals and Sanko added two. The Contractors won that game, 11–5, and Phil's line had nine goals.

We had another good line on that team. It was centered by Lloyd Basawa with Chuck Frayn and Leroy LaFleur on the wings. The remainder of the roster read like a Rome telephone directory. There was Jerry Bumbacco and Chet DePoli, Don Muscatello and Larry Simonini, Clem Giovanatti and Fuzzy Pezutto, Jim Rebellato and Harvey Barzanti, Lorne Grosso and Roger DeZardo. All good paisanos.

When Phil left home the following season to play junior hockey

Jim Sanko, Phil and Rich Lackowich: first line for Contractors.

Phil is flanked by Red DiPaulo (left) and Fraser Ryan.

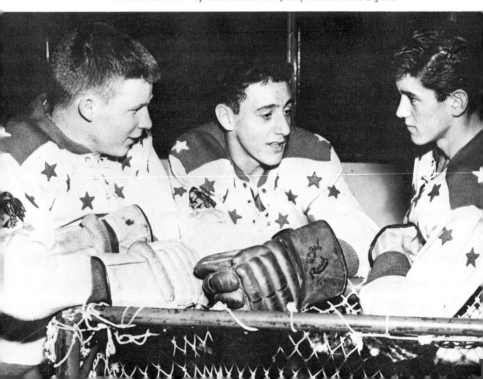

in Sarnia my whole outlook about hockey started to change. Maybe I was lonesome for Phil, I don't know. So after putting in another year of juvenile hockey — that would have been the 1960-61 season — I said the hell with it and concentrated on football.

I was then seventeen and I suppose I was going through all the emotional adjustments that face most boys of that age. I was a pretty frustrated kid. I didn't know then what I wanted to be, but I was sure I didn't have much of a future in hockey.

So I quit playing hockey for a whole season. I don't think I missed it, either, because I was becoming a football hero at St. Mary's.

In the fall of that same year some local people, including my dad and Angelo Bumbacco, formed a Junior A hockey team called the Soo Greyhounds. The coach was Abbie Naccarato, the same Abbie who refused to use me in those Juvenile playoffs three years earlier.

They joined forces and started bugging me about joining the team. By this time I was eighteen and still a mixed-up kid. Around the Soo I had a feeling people were calling me a quitter. Whether it was imagined or real, I don't know, but it bothered me.

"I'm not a quitter," I told my dad one day when the Greyhounds were being formed.

"I know you're not, son," he said. "But I don't want to influence you in any way. If you want to play hockey again, it has to be your decision and yours alone."

"Okay," I said, "I'm going to play for the Greyhounds. I'll never find out if I'm good enough for Junior A unless I try."

It was a decision I never regretted, of course. I had a good year with the Greyhounds that season and it helped me prove to myself that I had a future in hockey. But it was also a hectic year. I was then playing my final season of football at St. Mary's and playing Junior A hockey with the Greyhounds.

I would get out of school at three in the afternoon and practice football from three-thirty to four forty-five. I'd run and shower as quickly as I could, jump in a car and drive to the arena and dress for hockey. I used to bring a sandwich with me and eat it while I was getting into my goalie pads. Then, after hockey practice, I'd go home, do a little studying and fall into bed.

Once the football season ended, things eased up a little for me. Still, it was tough. The pressure is almost as bad in Junior A as it is in the pros. It's win, win, win. And when you don't win, look out.

I remember losing a Sunday afternoon game at North Bay that season. The round trip from the Soo to North Bay is almost five hundred fifty miles and we didn't get home until about four Monday morning. Everybody was dead tired, including Abbie Naccarato, who had to report for work that morning at seven. But what a coach he was.

"I'm taking you guys to the rink for a little practice," he said when we pulled into town.

"You've got to be kidding," I shouted.

He wasn't kidding. Abbie skated our butts off that morning. The sun was coming up when we finally got to bed.

There were other incidents I remember from that 1962-63 season with the Greyhounds. I was a little short-tempered and fought a lot. I had fights with rival players and even with my own teammates.

One day I got into a shouting match with a defenseman on our team. He was always causing trouble. We were in the locker room and he was bugging me pretty good so I jumped him and laid him out. I think it did him some good, too, because we didn't have any trouble with him after that.

Another time we were playing this team from Espanola. They had a big defenseman named Jim Currie — real bad news. He tried to jam me into the net and we got into a helluva brawl.

But there were lighter moments, too. Like the time we were playing a game in Sudbury and I halted the game because I thought I had lost one of my contact lenses. My dad came rushing down out of the stands with Angelo Bumbacco and the two of them got down on hands and knees on the ice, looking for the lens.

My dad's a pretty big man and watching him crawling along the ice was a comical sight.

"We've got to find that damn lens," he kept yelling to Angelo. "These contacts cost me one hundred twenty bucks."

Angelo, the manager of the Greyhounds, was just as concerned. He knew those were the only contacts I owned and we were battling

Sudbury for first place, so this was an important game. They couldn't afford to lose me or one of my lenses.

"We'll find the damn thing, Pat, don't worry," Angelo said.

By this time I was back in the dressing room and while fingering my eye I discovered what had happened to the lens. I hadn't lost it. It was still in my eye. But it had moved over into a corner of the eye and I thought it had popped.

I straightened it out myself, came back on the ice and told my dad about it. He was still down on his hands and knees. He looked up at me, turned a little red in the face and then laughed.

"Well, for cripes sake, get back in the game," he said.

We went on to win that day and when the season was over I was ready for college — and more hockey.

CHAPTER V

PENALTY-BOX FRACTURE

Phil Esposito's formal education ended after he had completed 3½ years of high school. After playing football during his final year at St. Mary's, he left home and entered a school of hard knocks — otherwise known as Canadian hockey's junior amateur ranks.

Looking back on my high school days now I often wonder how I ever escaped winding up as a truck driver. I was still an awkward kid in those days with doubtful athletic talent. While Tony was preparing himself for college, I was preparing myself for the life of a goof-off.

Even on the football field, I joked around a lot. Especially in practice. Our coach at St. Mary's was Father Pat LaLonde, a wonderful priest and an even greater man. He put up with an awful lot of nonsense from me.

There was one practice session we had when I was seventeen that I'll never forget. Father was working our tails off. Near the end of practice, most of us were standing around with our tongues hanging out, hoping he would quit. Then I decided to speak up. Big-mouth Phil.

"Father," I said, "I protest most vigorously this strenuous workout and your inhuman treatment."

That broke up the guys — and also the practice.

Every time I return home and run into Father LaLonde he remembers that day at practice. He will shake my hand, wink at me and say, "I protest most vigorously . . ."

We never won a game while I was playing football at St. Mary's

Phil kept them laughing when he played football at St. Mary's.

— mainly because of jerks like me. I played right end on offense and linebacker on defense. I wasn't much better as a pass-catcher, but I did like being a linebacker, probably because I loved to tackle guys.

Reno Candido and I teamed up on defense. I played right linebacker and he was middle linebacker. We were pretty tough, or thought we were. When I'd tackle a guy Reno would be there to throw a punch and vice-versa.

In one game, he threw a punch and I threw one almost simultaneously. You can guess what happened. The guy we had lined up ducked and we wound up hitting each other. What clowns! Reno and I were such wild-swinging guys that we got kicked out of two games that season for unsportsmanlike conduct.

It was obvious to most people — including myself — that I had no future in pro football. I wasn't even sure at that age I would be able to make it in pro hockey. And if some of the coaches I played under back in the Soo didn't show a little patience with me, maybe I wouldn't have made it.

Two of the men who helped me a great deal in those days were Richard Filek and Abbie Naccarato. Filek will admit to this day that he had some doubts about my hockey potential as a kid. I was a slow skater to begin with and I showed little improvement in that area as I was growing up.

But with Richard's help, I worked hard on my skating. He also taught me most of the finer points of playing center. He had me concentrate on handling the puck and setting up plays. I thrived on the fancy stuff, deking a defenseman one way and then going the other way.

Richard also helped me develop the quick wrist shot I use now, especially on drives from the slot. He had a good wrist shot himself, so I feel a little of his talent rubbed off on me.

He had one drill, though, I used to hate. It was strictly a defensive maneuver. He would show us how to face an onrushing puck-carrier, drop to one knee and block the shot with either the knee or the body or reach out with the stick and poke-check the puck.

There are some players who are great at this. Guys like Derek Sanderson or Eddie Westfall of the Bruins will try this when they are killing penalties. They're good at it. But not me. I don't do it any more. Defensemen and goalies get paid to stop the puck. Phil Esposito gets paid to score.

Abbie Naccarato worked hard with me, too, while I was playing juvenile hockey. He taught me many things, the most important being respect for your coach. He was the type of a man who demanded it and if you didn't show him respect you didn't play. It didn't matter to him if you were the star of the team or a bum. He was the boss and he wanted you to accept that.

One thing Abbie detested was shooting the puck against the boards in practice. He couldn't stand the noise. We knew this, of course, and we used to drive him crazy on occasion. We'd wait until he had his back turned, whack the puck off the boards, and then skate off, whistling and smirking a little.

I tried this one day in practice and Abbie went wild.

"Did you just shoot the puck against the boards?" he asked.

"Yeah, sure I did," I said. I was then seventeen and a real wise guy.

"Then get off the ice," Abbie hollered.

Man, was I teed off at him that day. But I knew he wasn't kidding, so I left the ice and after taking a shower I dressed and sat in the stands. My dad was there that day. I sat down alongside him, still fuming.

"Abbie was right in what he did, Phil," my dad said. "You shouldn't be such a hot head."

Of course he was right. I know that now. And, you know, after that incident I never shot the puck against the boards again until I got to the pros, where I've found the coaches are a little more lenient than Abbie Naccarato.

We had our share of fun, though, with Abbie. Thrills, too. Like that final season playing for him when we won the All-Ontario Juvenile "A" championship. I had four goals and three assists in one game against Owen Sound. This was in the spring of 1960. I had just turned eighteen and I figured I was ready for the big leagues.

I was doomed to more disappointment. I left home for the first time that September and failed to make the grade with the St. Catharines TeePees, a Junior "A" team then sponsored by the Chicago Black Hawks. So I wound up playing Junior "B" hockey in Sarnia, Ontario, with my old Soo linemates, Jimmy Sanko and

Richard Lackowich, and Chester DePoli, a defenseman from the Soo. The four of us lived together in a rooming house in Sarnia. We played two and sometimes three games a week and were paid the handsome sum of fifteen dollars a week. Chet DePoli was the only one among us who had a part-time job. He also owned a car — a 1956 Ford.

We were all a little lonesome, so we used to jump in Chet's car after a game at about midnight, drive all night to the Soo, spend a couple of days at home and then head back to Sarnia for the next game.

I enrolled at a Catholic high school in Sarnia shortly after joining the team and it was a disaster. I was then in the twelfth grade. I had missed the first six weeks of school and they were in the middle of an exam period when I got there. I just wasn't prepared for the tests, but the principal insisted I take them anyway.

The first exam I faced was in English. I didn't even try. I took the test paper and wrote across the top of it: "I don't know nothing," and signed my name. Just like that.

The principal of the school, a tough nun, called me into her office. I was playing the big shot, but she put me in my place right quick.

"Phil," she said, "I'm sorry but we don't want any hockey bums around here. Either you come here to study or you leave."

When she called me a hockey bum I really got mad.

I said, "Sister, I didn't come all this way from the Soo to go to school. If I wanted to go to school I'd have stayed home. I'm in Sarnia to play hockey, so I'm quitting your school."

I walked out of there and never returned. This was shortly after Christmas of 1960. I was afraid to tell my dad I had quit school because I figured he'd come and get me and drag me back to the Soo. So I let it hang for a couple of months and used the money he was sending me for school tuition to live on.

Naturally, I'm sorry now I didn't at least finish high school. If I had to do it over again, I'd work harder and study harder. My brother has it made now. He has his college degree and if he decides he'd like to go into teaching later, well, he can. When I quit hockey I'd like to have a job coaching in college, but maybe

I won't qualify. And it's all my fault. When I was a kid, who wanted school?

The chief schooling I got in Sarnia was how to play hockey, how to put the puck into the net. I learned pretty fast. I also learned what it was like traveling all over Ontario on a bus with the team. Our coach, Ollie Haddon, rarely traveled with us but he did permit us to take girls on the bus. They were sort of like Army camp followers.

We did a little boozing on the bus, too. We'd buy miniature bottles of liquor — we called them "Mickeys" — and mix the stuff with Cokes. We'd drink half of the bottle of Coke and then pour in the booze. We were mostly eighteen- and nineteen-year-olds, so it didn't take much to get us high. But the stuff also used to keep us warm on those damn cold nights in the bus.

Despite all the hell we raised, we still managed to play pretty good hockey. I got off to a flying start that year, scoring fifteen goals in my first ten games. Our team, the Sarnia Legionnaires, was in the Western Division of the Ontario Hockey Association Junior "B" league — a real high-scoring league.

Goals were a dime a dozen, or close to it. In my last regular-season game against London, I scored five goals and assisted on four others. I wound up with forty-seven goals and sixty-one assists for one hundred eight points. And that was for a thirty-two-game schedule.

But would you believe I lost the league scoring championship that year to Terry Crisp? He played for the St. Mary's Lincolns and in his final regular-season game against London he picked up twelve points and beat me out of the title, the little bugger.

At the end of the season I went back to driving a truck for my dad. Hey, I was some truck driver, believe me. I used to drive those ten-wheel babies. Loaded down with slag or plain junk the total payload would be maybe forty-five tons, but I handled that truck like it was a little old sedan.

That same summer of 1961 I got engaged to Linda Lavasseur. We had gone to school together, starting in public school, but we didn't start going steady until I came back from Sarnia. Here's how it happened:

I went to this party in the Soo with another girl and Linda showed up with my good friend, Jerry Bumbacco. Tony was there, too, with Marilyn, his sweetheart and now his wife.

We all had a few beers at the party and Jerry got wiped out. We had to carry him home. That left Linda without an escort. I was pretty stoned, too, but she permitted me to drive her home. When we got to the house, I tried to make a pass at Linda.

"Nobody gets out of my car without being kissed," I told her.

"Oh, no you don't," she said.

Then, as she reached for the door, I grabbed her by the back of the head and kissed her. She was mad as hell and ran into the house.

I really liked that girl and her spunk. I kept phoning her for the next four weeks, but she kept hanging up on me. Finally, I decided to give her an ultimatum over the phone.

"Linda, this is Phil," I said. "I'd like to date you, but if you refuse me this time I'll never ask again."

She asked me where we would go and I suggested the drive-in movie.

"Are you going to be as fresh as you were the last time I got in your car?" she asked.

"Of course not," I said. "That's why I want to take you out. I want to show you I'm not that kind of a guy."

So she accepted the invitation and it was the start of something big. I was a real gentleman through the whole stinking movie that night. I then took her home and never once tried to kiss her.

Later that summer we got engaged. Would you believe at seven-thirty in the morning while I was on my way to work? Honest. I stopped at her house, her mother came to the door, then Linda was there in front of me, sleepy-eyed and a little confused.

I said, "Linda, I'd like to give you this engagement ring. If you don't want it, I'll just take it back and that will be it."

Cripes, was she surprised. She didn't know what to say for a minute or two. I'm sure she wasn't fully awake, which maybe was a good thing for me. Anyway, she yawned and accepted the ring and I went off to work a very happy guy. Linda? I think she went back to bed.

At the end of August I left the Soo again for the Black Hawks' rookie camp near St. Catharines. I had ballooned to two hundred ten pounds that summer and was trying to skate off some of the fat at the rink when a guy hollered at me.

"Hey, Fatso," he said. "Come on over here."

It was Rudy Pilous, who then owned the St. Catharines Junior "A" team, which produced many, many players for the Black Hawks.

I skated over to Pilous and said, "You call me?"

"Yes," he said. "You want to make this team of mine?"

"Sure. What do I do?"

"Lose some weight," Pilous said. "Get down to two hundred pounds by the start of the exhibition season and you've got a job."

I was then nineteen years old, a little late to be starting in Junior "A", but I wanted that job, so I went on a starvation diet. It was tough. I'd watch the other guys eating hot dogs and drinking milk shakes and go nuts. I didn't eat between meals and at dinner I'd just have a piece of steak.

By the time we were ready to play our first exhibition game I was down to two hundred one — a pound over. I was wetting my pants because I figured Pilous would send me packing. But he offered me a contract and I signed it. The pay was better than Sarnia — fifty-seven fifty a week. My room and board was seventeen fifty, so that left me with forty dollars a week to spend, plus some extra money my dad sent me.

I didn't play in the first six exhibition games, though, so I started to get discouraged. Then Ray Cullen, one of our centers, got hurt and Ken Campbell, who was coaching the TeePees, named me as Cully's replacement. I scored five goals in a game against a Senior "A" team.

Looking back on that game now I get the willies. The day before I had gone to Campbell and told him if I wasn't used soon I was going home. I was worried about losing my seniority as a truck driver. Then I got the five goals and forgot all about the trucks.

Right there in St. Catharines the road opened up. I was on my way to the big leagues.

I saw my first NHL game while I was playing for St. Cats. It was a game between the Black Hawks and the Maple Leafs in

Toronto. Imagine, I was nineteen at the time and never before had attended a big-league game, although I had seen hundreds on television.

I made the trip from St. Catharines to Toronto with some of my teammates. The game was a sellout but we were able to buy standing-room tickets. While we were waiting for the game to start, I bought a program.

Now this is the real truth. They used to award prizes in those days to the fans, using the program numbers to determine the winners. Well, they announced my number and I almost died. I won an electric razor.

I've played a lot of games in the Maple Leaf Gardens since then and had my share of thrills, but nothing matched that night.

I think Chicago won the game, 6–2. The Black Hawks had players like Murray Balfour and Reg Fleming, Elmer Vasko and Glenn Hall, and, of course, Bobby Hull and Stan Mikita — fellows I would get to know more intimately a couple of years later.

On the trip back to St. Catharines that night all I talked about was Hull and Hall — and the electric shaver I had won.

That 1961-62 St. Catharines team should have won the Memorial Cup, which is awarded annually to Canada's top Junior "A" team. At least that's my feeling because we had some great players.

Roger Crozier was our goalie. On defense we had guys like Doug Jarrett, Brent Hughes, Billy Speer and Poul Popiel. They all made it to the NHL. And up front we had my old buddies from the Soo, Richard Lackowich and Jerry Bumbacco; Dennis Hull and Ken Hodge, Ray Cullen and John Brenneman, Duke Harris, and the Stanfield brothers, Jack and Fred.

I was battling for the scoring title when I broke my left wrist. It was a freak accident and one that caused me a little embarrassment. We were playing a game at Hamilton when I fell out of the penalty box.

Funny, right? But, damn, it wasn't funny to me. I had just finished serving a penalty and tried to jump over the sideboards. One of my skates caught and clumsy old Phil fell on the ice and landed on his wrist. I was in no shape for the playoffs, and that hurt. Hamilton eliminated us in a seven-game series and went on to win the Memorial Cup.

Once the playoffs were completed, I made my pro debut in my hometown with the Soo Thunderbirds, who were then playing in the old Eastern Professional Hockey league. They were affiliated with the Black Hawks, who wanted to get a look at me against the pros.

I had recently turned twenty and I still had a cast on my fractured wrist. It hampered me a lot and all I got was three assists during a six-game trial. One of those games was against the Kitchener Rangers. Rod Gilbert and Jean Ratelle were with Kitchener then and Red Sullivan was the player-coach. Sullivan didn't take long to introduce me to the tricks of an old pro.

We were matched against each other in a face-off. That little red-headed sneak won the draw, then he took the skates out from under me. He also speared me as I was going down.

Jim Farelli, who was playing for the Thunderbirds, came to my rescue. "Leave the kid alone, Red, or I'll cut your head off," he hollered at Sullivan.

Sully laughed and said, "The rookie's gotta learn."

Red remembered Farelli's warning, though. He didn't come close to touching me the rest of the game.

That was my introduction to the pros. I wore five different casts on my broken wrist that summer and was shook up when Dr. Bill Kelly, who was caring for me, said I'd be lucky to play hockey the following season. I was seized by more doubts, more worries.

CHAPTER VI

BRAVE IN ST. LOUIS

A salary of one hundred thousand dollars a year is not uncommon for superstars in a number of sports. It's still a relative rarity in hockey. Phil Esposito would one day reach that bracket. But in his rookie season as a pro in 1962-63 he was paid thirty-eight hundred dollars for seventy-one games.

Late in the summer of 1962 I was invited to the Chicago Black Hawks' training camp in St. Catharines, Ontario. Was I excited! The Black Hawks. Wow. All my previous doubts and worries were erased by that invitation.

I did face two problems, though, when I showed up at camp. First, I was out of shape, terribly out of shape. I wore a cast on my fractured left wrist for most of the summer and wasn't able to do anything except sit around and drink beer. The wrist healed nicely, but the rest of my body . . . well, I was just too damn fat. I had ballooned to two hundred twenty-five pounds.

And then I encountered a little trouble with Tommy Ivan, the general manager of the Black Hawks, when we met at St. Catharines to discuss my contract. On this particular day he had all the rookies lined up outside his room. I was one of the first he called.

I knew what I wanted in the way of money when I sat down in front of Tommy: a thousand dollar bonus and thirty-eight hundred for playing. I had only that one year of Junior "A" hockey behind me, but I didn't figure that was exorbitant.

"Phil," he said, "we're prepared to offer you five hundred dollars for signing and three thousand two hundred for playing."

"It's not enough," I said.

Ivan looked at me, gave me that fake smile and said:
"Look, that's the best we can do. Do you want to turn pro or not?"
"Not for that kind of money," I said.
"Okay, fine. Out the door. Send in the next player on line."
That's the way Ivan always operated. No nonsense, all business.
Sign or get out.

Although unsigned, I remained in the Hawks' camp for a few
more days and then was assigned to Syracuse of the Eastern League.
The club, coached by Gus Kyle, was training at Welland, only
about ten miles from St. Catharines.

The Hawks were running the Syracuse team and the day before
we broke camp, Ivan agreed to give me that three thousand eight
hundred dollar contract, plus a thousand dollar bonus for signing. I
sent the thousand to my dad as part payment for all he had given me
during my junior days. And knowing him, he never banked it. I'm
sure he returned most of it to me somewhere along the line.

Kyle was surprised that Ivan met my demands. "You really stuck
it to us, Phil, didn't you?" he said.

I didn't answer him, but that really burned me. Stuck it to
them, did I? I'd like to be still playing for them now so I could
really stick it to the whole Chicago organization. Maybe my brother
will one of these days. At least I hope so.

Gus Kyle, though, wasn't that bad a fellow. He did his best
with a bunch of pretty wild kids. I roomed with my old buddies
from the Soo, Richard Lackowich and Donnie Grosso. And when
the three of us went out we were usually joined by Nick Polano,
Murray Hall, Jack Turner and Duke Harris.

Kyle called us "The Magnificent Seven," or "The Chinese
Gamblers." He knew we were breaking training rules on him, but
he never cracked down too hard. "You're such nice quiet guys during
the day," he would say, "but when the lights come on, boy, do
you swing."

I have more stories to tell about old Gus. We once caught him
alone in the equipment room and locked the door. He banged and
banged on the door until we couldn't stand the noise any longer
and finally let him out. He was really fuming that day.

And I remember playing a game against Kingston when Gus
sent Grosso out on one shift and wouldn't let him off the ice.

Grosso was then in Gus' doghouse. Poor Donnie's tongue was hanging out at the end of the period. And he was so enraged he kicked over the players' bench and it landed on Kyle's foot.

Near mid-season, the Hawks decided to move the team from Syracuse, where fan support had been poor, to St. Louis. We left Syracuse in our cars on New Year's Eve and were supposed to drive directly to St. Louis. But Donnie, Richard, Nick and I decided to go home first. We drove all New Year's Eve and got into the Soo at around two in the morning.

The following day — January 2 — we resumed our trip to St. Louis in a red Oldsmobile. It took us two more days of steady driving. Then, without getting any sleep, we checked our stuff at a St. Louis hotel and went to the rink, where we had a game to play that night.

Kyle was fit to be tied when we finally showed up. "Welcome back, you buggers," he said. And, boy, did he work our butts off that night.

But no amount of hard work could help that hockey club. We won only thirteen games all season. Imagine that? Only thirteen victories in seventy-two games.

In the face of all those defeats, old Gus never lost his sense of humor. Our power play was so bad that when the other team was penalized, Gus would holler to the referee, "No, no, we decline it. We'll take the fifteen yards instead."

Kyle once handed me the shortest suspension in the history of hockey. We were at practice and I didn't feel like skating. Gus had a bad habit of sitting on the boards, smoking a cigarette and blowing the whistle for us to skate faster. I refused to speed up. He spotted me dogging it and told me, "Phil, get the hell out of here. You're suspended."

I was in the locker room getting undressed when he came in and said, "I want to see you in my office in five minutes." I still had my equipment on when I went to his office. We talked for a while and then he looked me in the eye and asked, "What's wrong with this club, Phil?"

That really threw me. I was a first-year pro. What could I tell him about his club? But the thing that got me is that never once did he mention the suspension. And when I got up to leave, he said, "Phil, get downstairs now, get your skates on and get back to practice." That was the end of the suspension.

I made one other visit to Kyle's office that I'll never forget. It was the day after our season had ended and I was looking for expense money to get home. I was feeling pretty chipper because, despite all the fooling around, I had put in a good season. I had scored thirty-six goals and fifty-four assists for ninety points. Gus cut me down a peg or two.

He said, "Phil, it's really been nice having you on the team. Now I want you to go home and keep yourself in good shape, eat the proper foods and don't do anything I wouldn't do."

Gus was easy on me. But I heard one story about how he told one of my teammates the same thing, and then added: "I want you to come back here next season and screw around with the broads, and drink booze and do every God-damned thing you did behind my back this season."

Good old Gus. He was one of the nicest fellows I ever met in hockey. He was my greatest booster and always treated me fairly. I was looking ahead to rejoining him the following season if the Hawks felt I needed another year of experience in the minors.

Linda and I were married that summer. The date was August 19, 1963. Father Pat LaLonde, who had been giving Linda instructions in the Catholic religion, married us at St. Jerome's Church in the Soo. Tony was the best man and his fiancée, Marilyn, was the maid of honor.

Tony and I both were in pretty bad shape that day. The night before I had a sort of bachelor's party at my father's house. All our old school buddies were there. They started pouring beer into me and got me pretty damn drunk.

I really had the shakes the morning of the wedding. I cut my face to ribbons trying to shave and it was covered with small pieces of toilet tissue which I was using to stop the bleeding.

The wedding was scheduled for eleven in the morning. All of us guys got to the church early and, damn, I was nervous waiting there for Linda to show up. At about five minutes before the hour, I remember turning to Tony and saying, "I'm going to give Linda a couple of more minutes. If she's not here by then, I'm blowing. I can't stand this any longer."

Linda finally made it to church about five minutes late, which I guess is par for the course.

A funny thing happened when Father LaLonde asked for the rings. It was a double-ring ceremony and Tony was carrying both in his pocket. He was still half in the bag and when he tried to put the rings on the tray his hands were shaking so bad he dropped them. They jiggled around on the floor and everybody started laughing. Even shaky Tony was laughing.

Linda and I honeymooned in Florida. We made the trip in a Chevy convertible — a big mistake because it was so damn hot. The night we checked into a Miami Beach hotel I bought a bottle of champagne. Linda refused to drink any of it, so I got mad and finished the whole bottle. I was real bombed when I decided on taking a midnight swim. I walked into the ocean with my clothes on and, man, did that sober me up.

A few days later we headed for St. Petersburg on the west coast of Florida. That was a wild ride. I was hitting about a hundred miles an hour most of the way.

We had a helluva time in St. Pete, then headed home. We made stops at St. Louis and Chicago. By the time we got back to the Soo it was time for me to report again to the Hawks' camp at St. Catharines.

Chico Maki, who had put in his first full season with the Hawks the previous year, told me I was a cinch to make the big club. But I wasn't so sure. The Hawks must have felt the same way because I was back with Gus Kyle and the St. Louis Braves at the start of the 1963-64 season.

This was an entirely different team from the one I had played on the previous season. Jack McCartan, who had a shot with the New York Rangers after helping the United States team win the 1960 Olympic hockey championship, was our goalie. On defense, we had Jack Hendrickson, Pete Ford, Poul Popiel and Lloyd Haddon.

We were solid at center where Ray Cullen, Eric Sutcliffe and I held down that position. And our wingers included Al (Boom Boom) Caron, Ben Greco, John Brenneman, Duke Harris, Jack Stanfield and Bert Fizzell.

We won more games by Christmas than we had the entire

previous season and were battling Omaha for first place in the Central League. Caron got off to a fantastic start. He had thirty-seven goals in the Braves' first thirty-four games. He finished that season with an incredible seventy-seven goals.

I have often been asked why a goal-scorer like Caron never made it in the National League. He did play briefly with Montreal and California but I feel he just wasn't fast enough. He was a very poor skater. But he could shoot the puck like nobody I've ever seen, except Bobby Hull. In one game against Omaha, I saw Caron beat Cesare Maniago with a shot from the red line. The shot hit the post and still went in; that's how hard it was.

McCartan, like Caron, was a great minor-league player. And the reason he never made it back to the Rangers or some other National League team was because he, too, was a poor skater. Now that might sound silly in discussing a goalie, but I feel a goalie also has to be a good skater.

It all comes down to balance, quickness and agility. You have to have strong ankles to jump up and down on your skates and move from one side to another. I don't think Jack McCartan had that. He also looked good on tough shots and then would fan on easy shots.

When the NHL expanded, I guess Jack felt he would make it back. But he was then over thirty years old and no club was willing to risk big money on him. It's too bad, too, because I always liked him. I didn't like the cigars he smoked, though. On some of those long bus trips from St. Louis to Omaha, I used to hide Jack's cigars and he'd go out of his skull looking for them. And sometimes when he'd fall asleep with a cigar in his mouth, I used to get a pair of scissors and cut off the ends. Boy, he'd get teed off at that.

As the season progressed and my hockey playing improved, the St. Louis fans were beginning to treat me like a hero. I got one of my greatest thrills in a game against Omaha at the St. Louis Arena. We had two men in the penalty box and I was sent out to help kill the penalties. I picked up a loose puck just inside the blue line, got by two guys, and went in alone. I pulled Maniago out of the goal with a good fake and put it in.

In those days, before St. Louis joined the National League, when five thousand or six thousand fans showed up at the Arena it was a helluva crowd. There were probably less people on hand for that game, but they gave me a standing ovation.

I'll never forget that night.

I'll also never forget the night shortly afterwards when I was called up by the Black Hawks.

CHAPTER VII

ROOKIE IN THE HEM LINE

*Black Hawk fans weren't ready to give Phil
Esposito the keys to the city when he showed up in
Chicago in early 1964. In fact, there were some who
asked "Phil Who?" when he was called up from
St. Louis.*

You know that old gag about the wife being the last to know?
In the case of my call-up by the Black Hawks it seemed I was the
last to get the news. Linda was one of the first.

It was January 14, 1964, and I was in St. Paul, Minnesota, with
my St. Louis teammates. We were scheduled to play the St. Paul
Rangers the following night. I was a little concerned about Linda —
she had only recently discovered she was pregnant — so I phoned
her in St. Louis.

"What's going on, Phil?" she asked.

"Nothing, Linda. Why do you ask?"

"I heard on the radio here that the Black Hawks are calling
you up."

"You're kidding," I said. "Sit tight. I'll call you right back."

I hung up the phone and dashed off to see Gus Kyle. I located
him in his hotel room.

"I just heard the Hawks are thinking of bringing me up," I
said. "What gives, Gus? I've got a wife at home pregnant. I want
to know the truth."

"Okay, okay," Kyle said. "I wasn't going to tell you until
tomorrow, but after tomorrow night's game you're supposed to
head for Montreal and join the Black Hawks."

Terrific. I was on my way to the big leagues. I called Linda again and gave her the official news. Murray Hall, who had played with me in St. Louis the previous year, wasn't going too well with the Black Hawks. He had only two goals in twenty-four games. So he was being shipped back to the Braves and I would replace him on the Black Hawks' roster.

I left the St. Louis team with pretty good credentials. I had been leading the Central League in scoring for most of the season. In my final game against St. Paul, I scored two goals in the Braves' 7–3 victory. That gave me twenty-four goals and seventy-five points in forty-two games.

On Thursday morning, January 16, I took off for Montreal, stopping off at Chicago to change planes. I got into Montreal at six that night and went straight to the Forum. Billy Reay greeted me and told me to get dressed. "We might need you tonight," he said. It wasn't until that moment that I realized I hadn't eaten all day. Hell, what man could eat when he's about to make his major-league debut? And against the Montreal Canadiens.

Reay gave me a fast baptism. I went out for one shift in the first period, then Chico Maki drew a ten-minute misconduct penalty. I played the second period on a line with Ron Murphy and Eric Nesterenko. What a thrill that was. But, damn, I was pretty awful. I couldn't keep up with anybody and never got a shot on goal.

And I guess I was a little weak from not eating that day. I remember being checked by somebody, I can't recall who it was, and I went down like a ton of bricks.

My NHL debut wasn't anything to write home about.

Reay didn't use me in the next game and I was beginning to worry about whether I belonged in the NHL. And then there was the question of money. When the Hawks called me up they signed me to a seventy-five hundred dollar contract — the NHL minimum at the time. My salary at St. Louis was six thousand, but I had a bonus arrangement for goals, points, etc., so that I stood to earn maybe another seven thousand in bonus money. I was taking a cut in salary to play in the big leagues!

I started to feel a little better after I scored my first NHL goal. It came on January 25, 1964, ten days after my call-up, and was scored against the Red Wings at Detroit. I was centering a line for Bobby Hull and Reg Fleming that night.

Fleming did a great job setting up the goal. He had the puck near the red line and I skated between two Detroit defensemen — Bill Gadsby and Doug Barkley, I believe. Reggie fed me a perfect lead pass and I went in alone on Terry Sawchuk. I faked Terry to the right and he dropped to one knee. My shot flew over his right shoulder and into the net.

When I was growing up back in the Soo I used to listen to the games from Toronto and wonder what it would be like to fire a puck at Terry Sawchuk. Now I knew. I had beaten a boyhood idol for my first NHL goal. Cripes, what a thrill.

I came down off cloud nine later as Reay used me less and less. I finally went to Tommy Ivan, the same man I had quarreled with over my contract back at St. Catharines, and asked to be sent back to St. Louis.

"My wife is still back in St. Louis," I told Ivan. "Either I go back or you let me bring her to Chicago."

Ivan didn't quarrel with me this time. "Then bring your wife to Chicago," he said. "You're going to be here a while."

Now I was happy again. Linda joined me in Chicago and we rented an apartment in Hillside. It was the same apartment, by the way, that Tony and Marilyn would rent during my brother's first year with the Black Hawks.

During those early days with Chicago I was treated like any other rookie — with disdain. They all seemed pleasant enough when I first joined the club, but after that only three or four guys would bother talking to me. Bobby Hull was one of them. He's the greatest guy who ever lived. And, of course, Chico Maki. He is probably my best friend, next to Tony and Fred Stanfield.

Stan Mikita didn't treat me too well. He does now. But in those days we didn't hit it off. I don't know why either. Maybe I was jealous. I was a centerman and he was the best. We also had entirely different temperaments. I don't think Stan meant some of the things he said or some of the insults he threw at me. There are some people in this world who can call me "Wop" and it doesn't bother me. When Stan used that word it used to drive me nuts. I wanted to bust him right in the head.

Ron Murphy and I hit it off well from the moment I joined the Hawks. We later were linemates with the Bruins. On some days when the Hawks were supposed to be practicing, most of the regulars would take off, leaving behind the "Scrubeenies," guys like Fleming, Nesterenko, Murray Balfour and myself. And, oh yes, Johnny McKenzie. Pie Face was just breaking in there, too. We all wore black sweaters and Murphy called us the "Black Aces." We weren't really aces, however. I know I wasn't. I was having trouble with my skating. Reay used to watch me in practice and say, "Phil, you're a step behind." After a while it became a half step. So I kept working on my skating in practice. Then one day Billy came to me and said, "Phil, your skating has really improved. I think you've caught up with the other guys."

Still, Reay refused to use me on regular shifts. I finished the regular season with three goals in twenty-seven games. No ball of fire, eh? That's what some of the Chicago reporters started to write and it really teed me off.

How could I strut my stuff when I wasn't getting the ice time? This doesn't show in the record books, but in many of those twenty-seven games I'd be on for only one shift. Sometimes two shifts. I never got a chance to play a full game. Chico Maki, Stan Mikita and Billy Hay were the regular centers. I was just there to watch. But how can you learn by sitting on the bench and watching? It got awfully frustrating.

I suffered more frustration in the playoffs against Detroit. I dressed for the first three games and didn't get a chance to do anything as the Hawks lost all three. For the fourth game, Reay decided to dress McKenzie in my place. After our pre-game meeting that day, I went back to our apartment and told Linda to pack our bags.

"There's no way in the world we're going to win," I said. "There's no spirit left on the club. So get ready, Linda, and tomorrow we'll head home."

The Red Wings swept us out of the playoffs that night. Linda and I were back home in the Soo the following night.

As I sat around home that summer I became convinced that being called up by the Hawks in the middle of the season was jeopardizing my career. I know Reay and Ivan thought they were doing me a favor. But it hurt my pride to sit on the bench and it also cost me money — the bonus money I would have gotten if

I had remained in St. Louis.

A little happiness finally returned to my life that summer when Linda gave birth to our first child, Laurie. It was August 14, 1964. The night before I was at Jerry Bumbacco's house, playing cards, when Linda suffered her first labor pains. She came to me and said, "Phil, it's getting close. You better take me to the hospital."

I remember I had a helluva hand at the time. I wanted to win that pot. "Please wait, Linda," I said. "Just a couple of minutes until I finish this hand."

What a wife I have. She waited until I won the hand, then I took her to the hospital. Laurie was born the next morning.

I showed up at the Hawks' training camp in the fall wondering if I would be back riding the bench. But I soon learned that Billy Reay had big plans for me. He started out by using me and Chico Maki as penalty killers in exhibition games. We did a good job and this impressed Billy. I've always liked killing penalties. It's not as much fun as scoring goals, but I like doing it.

Once the season started, Reay made another big move. He switched Chico to right wing and I took over Chico's center spot on the third line. The other regular centers were Mikita and Hay. Fred Stanfield joined us and was made the alternate center, taking over my old job. So at the age of twenty-two, with two years of pro hockey behind me, I had finally become a regular in the NHL.

In our opening game of the 1964-65 season against the Boston Bruins I scored a goal and an assist in a 3–0 victory. That gave me almost half the points I had totaled in my rookie season (five). A good start.

The goal was scored against Ed Johnston, now one of my teammates and a good pal. I was killing a penalty with Maki when Chico fed me a pass. In rushing my shot, I only caught a piece of the puck and it barely trickled in. I kidded Johnston about it later. "That was my changeup," I said. I have to admit now that in my years in the league I've scored quite a few goals on freaky changeups like that.

Dennis Hull broke in as a regular in that same game and looked impressive. In fact, Dennis has always impressed me. He's strong and tough. Not tough to the point where he will maim a guy, but he's tough enough. And I sometimes think his shot is as hard or

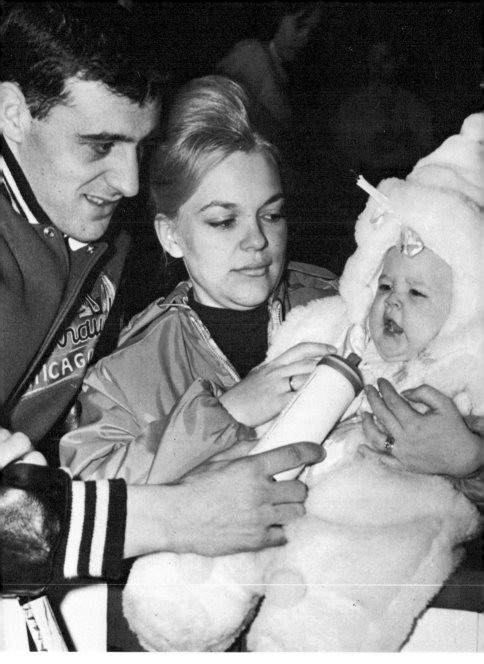

Phil gets credit for an assist as wife Linda holds daughter Laurie.

maybe harder than his brother Bobby's.

Dennis had only one fault in those days. He used to fall all the time. He'd go into a corner with the puck and fall down. I never could figure out why. I think to this day he doesn't know. Maybe it was because he was so young — he was in his teens at the time — and he had trouble maintaining proper balance.

Dennis and I have remained very close to this day. We have gone on vacations with our wives to Acapulco and Las Vegas, and have always had a ball. I consider Dennis and Doug Jarrett two of the nuttiest guys in hockey, and you must remember we have our own share of nuts in Boston.

After we had played about twenty games during the 1964-65 season, Reay shook up our forward lines. We were in a slump when we came into New York to play the Rangers at the old Madison Square Garden. Before the game, Billy came into the dressing room and said, "We're having a little trouble so we're going to make some changes." He looked at me and said, "Phil, you center for Chico and Bobby." Then he took Hay off Bobby Hull's line and put him between Murphy and Nesterenko.

That was how the "HEM Line" of Hull, Esposito and Maki was formed.

We went out that night and creamed the Rangers, 6–1. Bobby and Chico each got two goals and I got one. After the game, Reay told some New York reporters he was delighted with his new line. "They checked and moved the puck around like they've been playing together for years," Billy said.

Bobby, Chico and I did hit it off well. We went on to win thirteen games in a row. I think I got ten goals in those thirteen games and Bobby got fifteen. Chico got only four but he wasn't expected to score. He was the digger and the worker, the big assist man and the backchecker.

Reay used to take Chico aside and tell him not to worry about goals. "Chico," he would say, "you're the backchecker. Don't forget that."

That was the big thing with Reay. It probably still is. He's the only coach I know who would designate one man on a line to backcheck. Before a game, he'd go down the line and say, "Eric, you backcheck," and "Chico, I want you to backcheck." I figured

Chico Maki, Phil and Bobby Hull formed HEM Line for Chicago.

it was good strategy.

The one guy I felt sorry for when the HEM Line was formed was Billy Hay. He had lost his job, as Bobby Hull's partner, to me. I went to him because I didn't want him to be angry at me. "What's the matter with you?" he said. "Billy's the coach and he knows what he's doing. We're out to win, right? So forget it, rook." I thought that was great and I've never forgotten Billy Hay. He had a wonderful attitude and great team spirit.

About midway through the season, I was scoring quite a few goals and before long some of the defensemen in the league decided to test me. Gary Bergman of the Detroit Red Wings was one of them. One night we went into a corner together and he used his stick on me. I came out of the corner punching.

Now, I've never been much of a fighter. But neither is Bergman. Ha! He won't like me for that. Anyway, I think I got a draw in that one.

I finished the regular season with twenty-three goals and thirty-two assists for fifty-five points. That was good enough to earn me tenth place among the league's top scorers. Pretty good credentials, right? But I didn't qualify for the rookie-of-the-year award because of the twenty-seven games I had dressed for the previous year. That was seven games over the limit. The rookie award went to Roger Crozier, and I was a little peeved over that.

In the opening round of the 1965 Stanley Cup playoffs, we pulled off quite an upset by eliminating the Red Wings. They had won the regular-season championship while the Black Hawks finished third. I remember that series, though, for another reason. It involved a celebration in a Detroit hotel.

Before the seventh and decisive game in Detroit, Billy Reay had come into the dressing room and said, "If you guys win tonight, I'll buy the beer." We went out on the ice and skated like mad. We beat the Red Wings, but I don't remember Billy springing for the beer. He couldn't have because we went to a bar after the game, bought our own beer and brought it back to the hotel.

While we were out, a large family came to the hotel and needed a suite. Reay gave up his suite and got a room next door to us. We were unaware of this when we got back to the hotel.

Chico Maki was with us and Bobby Hull and Ken Hodge and

Fred Stanfield. We were really having a ball, drinking beer and heaving the empty cans against the wall. In the course of the celebration, somebody mentioned Reay and we started cursing him. The next day I showed up at the airport wearing sunglasses to hide my bleary eyes. Reay saw me with the shades on and said, "Why don't you take those things off?"

"If I did that I'd bleed all over you," I said.

He looked at me and in his best sarcastic voice said, "Yeah, I believe it."

We went on to Montreal and at a team meeting before our opening game against the Canadiens in the final round, Reay let me in on a little secret.

He said, "Esposito, I had the room next to you in Detroit and I heard everything you guys said."

That was an embarrassing moment. So was the final series against the Canadiens. It went the limit, seven games. In the first six games Reay used me, Chico and Bobby against the Jean Beliveau line. We had Beliveau mumbling to himself. He couldn't do anything.

Then, just before we went out to play the final game Reay decided on a switch. He called to Mikita and said, "Stan, your line starts tonight."

I was dumbfounded. So were Bobby and Chico. We had started against the Beliveau line in the sixth game and won it to tie the series. And in Reay's book of strategy the line that started a winning game always started the next one. To this day I don't know why Billy switched.

The move boomeranged on him when Beliveau scored after only fourteen seconds. Then Montreal got another a minute later. I think it was scored by Dick Duff. We were trailing, 2–0, before our line got on the ice.

The Canadiens added two more in that first period and won the game and the Stanley Cup, 4–0. It was the first one by Beliveau that really broke our backs. Man, was I mad. I'm not blaming Mikita's line, just Billy Reay. His move in switching assignments was a little irregular.

I suppose he wanted to go with a more experienced center like Mikita and that was his prerogative. But it turned out to be a mistake and Billy Reay should take the blame.

Montreal's Gump Worsley shut out Phil and Chicago in Cup finale.

CHAPTER VIII

BURYING THE CURSE
OF MULDOON

Phil Esposito never shared the sentiments of the songwriter who called Chicago a "wonderful town." He liked the fans but couldn't get along with the Black Hawks' management — namely coach Billy Reay and general manager Tommy Ivan.

Two completely unrelated incidents in 1965 left me wondering about my future with the Black Hawks. The first occurred in an exhibition game against the Detroit Red Wings prior to the start of the 1965-66 season.

Bryan Watson, that little pest, was playing for the Red Wings then. He had been acquired by the Hawks from the Montreal Canadiens a day before the annual draft meetings in June of that year. When the Hawks failed to find room for him on their protected list, the Red Wings drafted him. Now I guess he wanted to show the Hawks they had made a mistake in letting him get away.

In this particular tune-up game, most of the players were just going through the motions. After all, nobody wants to get hurt before the season starts. Watson had other ideas. He's always been good with his elbows and he used one on me after bouncing me into the boards.

I got sore and called him a "dirty little bastard." He retaliated by calling me a "dirty Wop." That did it. We started to bang away at each other pretty good. I can honestly say it was one of the few fights I won in pro hockey. But it was a costly victory. One of my punches caught Watson high on the temple and I broke my right hand.

That finished me for the rest of the exhibition season. The club didn't want me to play. I wanted to, but how could I play with a damn cast on my hand? I had no power in that hand and it hurt like hell.

I missed the season opener, then came back for the second game. It was murder. I played maybe four or five games while still wearing the cast. I finally took it off and went another eight games without scoring.

This was when I think Billy Reay started to get dissatisfied with me. Sometime in November, while I was still shaking off the effects of that broken hand, he demoted me to left wing on a line with Stan Mikita and Len Lunde. What a mistake that was. I was a poor left winger and, besides, Mikita and I didn't hit it off well. Reay did it to shake me up, but his experiment didn't last long. He put me back centering for Bobby Hull and Chico Maki after a few games and we started to roll.

Now we come to the second incident that helped grease the skids for me in Chicago. Chico and I missed a practice in Toronto and were fined one hundred dollars apiece.

The true story of how we missed that practice has never been told. Now's the time to tell it.

The previous night, Chico and I were in our room at the Royal York Hotel in Toronto well in advance of the eleven o'clock curfew. We couldn't sleep, so we sneaked out of the hotel and went to a nearby joint for a few beers.

We were back in our hotel room by twelve forty-five. We watched television for awhile and then fell asleep. The next thing I remember is the phone ringing. It was Johnny Morasco, an old friend from back home.

"What the hell's the idea of calling me now, Johnny?" I said. "It's still dark out."

"Dark, hell," Johnny said. "It's two-thirty in the afternoon."

I almost fell out of bed. Chico had pulled the blinds before he had gone to sleep, which explained the darkened room. I checked my watch and, sure enough, it was two-thirty. Our practice had been scheduled for two.

I went back to the phone, thanked Johnny for waking me and hung up. Then I woke up Chico. He was just as shocked as I was.

"What happened?" he kept mumbling. "What the hell happened?"

"You closed the damn blinds, that's what happened," I said.
"If you had let some light shine in the room maybe it would have
wakened us."

We dressed in less than five minutes and really scooted to the
Maple Leaf Gardens. Practice was almost over. Now it was Reay's
turn to ask questions.

"Okay, wise guys, what happened?"

"Billy, you won't believe this, but we overslept," I said.

"Past two o'clock? Is that true, Chico?"

"Yes, it's true," Chico said.

I don't think Reay would have believed me, but he accepted
Chico's word because they have always been good friends.

The hundred dollar fines weren't too bad. What annoyed me
was that a reporter from the Soo was in Toronto at the time. He
heard about us missing practice and, of course, it wound up in
the paper back home. But he never got the true story of how we
overslept.

Reay started getting on me after that incident. He kept telling
people that I wasn't aggressive enough. He'd be talking to a
reporter about me and he'd say, "I wish Phil had Mikita's attitude.
Stan had it tough when he was growing up." He was hinting that
I had everything fed to me on a silver spoon, which wasn't true,
although I was fortunate in having parents who made a lot of
sacrifices for me.

Stan Mikita did have it tough. His folks were in a concentration
camp. When he came to Canada from Czechoslovakia as a kid he
ran into a lot of discrimination. Look, I hand it to the man. He
had to fight his way to the top.

But who is to say what the right attitude in hockey is supposed
to be? Who's to say what the right attitude in life is? Not Billy
Reay. I told him that one day.

"Why should you be the judge of the way I approach this game,
Billy?" I said. "What if I don't want to adopt your attitude?"

"Well," he said, "you won't play hockey too long."

"Bullshit," I said. "I disagree with you. A man can play hockey
and be a nice guy, too."

That ended our conversation. On this subject, I feel the same
way today. Sometimes you have to be dirty. I know that. There are

times when you have to stand up for your rights and fight. I've had only about a half dozen good fights in the NHL. I haven't won many of them, but I've fought. I've also used my stick with the best of them and got a stick in return.

(Years later, after I'd gone to Boston, Mikita speared me while I was standing in front of the net in a playoff game. It really bothered me, but I waited for the right moment to get my revenge. It happened later in the game in front of the Chicago bench. Stan was looking for a pass and I reefed him, gave him a spear. I got him right in the stomach and down he went, right in front of Reay. Billy was more upset over it than Stan. "Cheap-shot artist," he hollered. I laughed in his face. "Buzz off, Billy. How's that for attitude?")

At about that same time in my career, Reay had no confidence in me on faceoffs. As most hockey fans know, many games are won or lost on the guy who can outdraw his opponent in such duels. You stand there face-to-face with your opponent, the puck is dropped by the linesman and it's up to you to beat him to the draw and clear the puck to a teammate. This is one of the primary jobs of a center.

In the NHL today, we have many great faceoff men. Phil Goyette, the former New York Ranger center who wound up with Buffalo in the expansion draft, has always been one of the best. So is Derek Sanderson. I've seen games when Derek has won fourteen or fifteen straight faceoffs. Other good faceoff men are Jean Ratelle of the Rangers, Danny O'Shea of Chicago, Jean Beliveau of Montreal, Red Berenson of Detroit and Stan Mikita.

During that 1965-66 season with Chicago, Reay rarely used me on important faceoffs. The job usually went to Mikita or Bill Hay. Maybe, I wasn't great at the job then, but how was I going to learn if I never got the chance?

The truth of the matter is that Reay's lack of confidence in me helped to shatter my own confidence. But despite him and the poor start I had because of the broken hand, I finished the regular season with twenty-seven goals.

The greatest memory I have of that season was helping Bobby Hull break Rocket Richard's fifty-goal record. Bobby finished with fifty-four. But he should have been credited with fifty-five. Why?

I'll tell you.

We were playing a game against the Bruins at Chicago when Bobby got his forty-ninth. He also got his fiftieth that night by deflecting one of my shots past goalie Bernie Parent. But Bobby refused to accept it. I went to Bobby and said, "Hey, didn't you get your stick on that shot?" He said, "Naw, Phil, I just grazed it. It was going in anyway. It's your goal."

Bobby Hull. What a man. A few nights later he got his official fiftieth and then his fifty-first to break Richard's record. I remember how nervous Bobby was leading up to that record. And the excitement. You could feel it every time we stepped on the ice. When Bobby finally broke the record, we all mobbed him and the crowd went wild. I had never heard an ovation like that.

My relationship with Bobby is based on complete respect. I think, though, that Bobby was a lonely man when I was with Chicago. Chico Maki and I became close friends with Bobby because I feel he wanted it to happen. We were kind of leery of associating with a superstar. Maybe he'll resent this, but Bobby made friends with us. This is the type of guy he was then and is today. He always treated me great and I've treated him the same way.

You read all this nonsense about Bobby being an adonis and a skirt-chaser but very little of it is true. I know. I used to room with him on the road on occasions and the phone would be ringing constantly. Girls would be calling him and he'd be kidding them and when he grew tired of that he'd say, "Thanks for calling but please don't bother me." That's the truth.

I went into the 1966-67 season with the Hawks feeling pretty much the way I had the previous season: my days in Chicago were numbered. I was still having trouble with management. But now I had another problem. The Chicago writers were getting on my back.

The two writers who gave me the most trouble were Chip Magnus and Dan Moulton. Moulton was the guy who first called me a "garbage collector." He was interviewing me one day and asked, "How do you like standing around picking up garbage?" I didn't know what he was talking about and told him so.

Rangers' Bob Nevin scrambles with Phil as Denis DeJordy watches.
Bobby Hull, left, teams with Phil against Montreal's Ted Harris.

"Oh, you know," he said. "You're great at scoring goals on Hull's rebounds."

This shook me up and I started to get angry.

"I get paid to score goals," I said. "If it means I've got to garbage-collect, then that's what I do."

The next day, Moulton's paper carried a big headline: "Phil Esposito Is Hawk Garbage Collector."

That was the beginning of something I have had to live with throughout my pro hockey career. I go into rinks today and people still call me a garbage collector. It doesn't matter where it is. Philadelphia, New York, Chicago. They still give me that crap.

I think it's unfair. I really do. I get a lot of good goals now where I have to work like hell. And sometimes I get the garbage, which are mainly rebounds in front of the net. But you have to take those, too, because many games are won on rebounds.

The player who is quick in front of the net is going to win. If a defenseman is quicker than I am, he is going to clear the puck before I get a chance to shoot it. My job is to beat him — and the goalie. And don't forget, just by moving into that area we call the "slot" — actually it should be called "Death Valley" — I take a helluva lot of punishment. I take a lot of raps on my back and my head and my legs trying to beat the defenseman to the puck.

But they still call me a "garbage collector," and I can blame that on Dan Moulton. Whenever the Hawks lost a game he'd say it was my fault or Elmer Vasko's. We were his whipping boys. Maybe, Billy Reay or Tommy Ivan fed him that crap to get us going. I don't know, but it was unfair.

At any rate, the bad publicity I was getting in Chicago really bugged me. I still managed to score twenty-one goals in that 1966-67 season and the Black Hawks won their first pennant. We had finally buried the curse of Peter Muldoon, the first coach of the Hawks who had predicted when he was fired in 1927 that "this team will never finish in first place."

This was probably the greatest team I ever played for. You might consider that statement shocking, but stop and consider the men we had on that Chicago team. Man for man, they were great.

The goalies were Glenn Hall and Denis DeJordy, who shared the Vezina Trophy that season. On defense we had Pierre Pilote, who was then an All-Star, and Matt Ravlich, who had his best year ever, plus Doug Jarrett and Pat Stapleton. Up front, we had Stan Mikita and Bobby Hull and Ken Wharram, who were named to the All-Star first team. Dennis Hull had a great year and so did Doug Mohns and Eric Nesterenko and Chico Maki. It was one helluva team.

Our celebration after we finished first — by seventeen damn points — was unreal. I got so drunk I went up to Tommy Ivan at the champagne party and really laid it to him. I had always been wary of Tommy. What the hell, let's admit it: I was frightened of him. But the champagne gave me some false bravery.

"Tommy," I said, "you've got a dynasty building here. Please don't screw it up."

Bobby Hull heard me talking to Ivan and tried to lead me to the door. But I wouldn't go. I was bombed.

"Let me say what I've got to say, Bobby," I kept repeating. "You know Tommy's going to screw it up."

Bobby wrapped one of those big arms of his around me and whispered, "Phil, let's get the hell out of here. You've said enough already."

He was right. I had said too much.

My days in Chicago now were surely numbered, and it was my own fault.

CHAPTER IX

BEER ON ICE

The number of young Canadian hockey players matriculating at United States colleges has been rising fast in recent years. They travel south from their homes in Manitoba and Saskatchewan, Ontario and Quebec to further their education at little or no cost, bartering their talent as hockey players for full scholarship offers. That's how Tony Esposito wound up at Michigan Tech.

My initial introduction to Michigan Tech and its hockey coach, John MacInnes, was not especially pleasant. I wasn't welcomed with open arms. But perhaps I was lucky to get a scholarship there in those days.

Actually, my best high school sport was football. I was a running back at St. Mary's in the Soo and scored my share of touchdowns. A Catholic university in the Eastern United States — I can't even remember its name now — offered me a football scholarship and Michigan Tech offered me a hockey scholarship.

Those were the only two I received. I wasn't interested in playing college football because I figured I wasn't big enough. I had good speed — I won medals in track while I was in high school — but at five feet, eleven inches and one hundred eighty-five pounds I didn't feel I could take the pounding you get in big-time college football.

I felt I could develop into a better hockey player. I had played that one year of junior hockey and was fairly successful. So in September of 1963 I headed for Michigan Tech in Houghton, which is only about two hundred seventy-five miles from the Soo.

Coach MacInnes had promised me a full scholarship that summer, but when I showed up at Tech they started to give me a bit of a run-around. There was another goalie coming in from the West — his name was Rick Best from Winnipeg — and it soon became apparent that MacInnes was counting on him as his top prospect. At the time, he didn't seem to have any big plans for me.

One day before the start of practice for the freshman team, MacInnes called me in to discuss my scholarship. He hemmed and hawed for awhile and then said, "Tony, we're not going to be able to give you the full scholarship until you prove you can make the team." What a shock that was.

I was ready to tell MacInnes what he could do with his hockey team and Michigan Tech, then decided against it. What the hell, if I went home I'd probably wind up driving a truck for my father.

After my second practice with the freshman team, MacInnes called me in for another chat. "Tony," he said, "we've changed our minds about you. We're prepared to cover all your expenses here, including room and board."

"All right," I said. "That's more like it, and thanks."

So now I was really embarked on a college career with a full scholarship — a free ride for four years. I was damn glad I hadn't decided to return to the Soo.

Houghton, I must admit, is a pretty decent college town — provided you don't mind a little snow. They get about two hundred fifty inches of the stuff every winter. And they never plow the sidewalks. You walk along on mounds of snow where the sidewalks are buried and look down at the cars in the street. It's a funny sensation.

It wasn't that cold there. At least, it didn't seem too cold to a guy like me from the Soo. The winter temperature averaged about ten above, but because the town is located in a sort of valley, protecting it from the wind, it never got too rough.

This is a real small town, by the way. The total population is about ten thousand, and it's ninety miles west of Marquette, Michigan, which is the closest city to Houghton.

When I first arrived at Michigan Tech I was nineteen years old and I had a chip on my shoulder, a real chip. But I really grew up in the next four years.

The biggest trouble I encountered as a freshman was attempting to adjust to college life. It wasn't easy. Maybe it's because I was too interested in fun-seeking and beer-drinking.

Even the housing we had during my first three years at Michigan Tech sort of contributed to the fun. They had barracks for the hockey players to live in. We used to have seven or eight of us in the barracks and we could do what we wanted.

They were sort of like old Army barracks — and I do mean old. Geez, they were wrecks. But they were homey, too, in a sense. Not like a house, of course, but we got used to living there and we didn't want to live anywhere else.

We lived two to a room. In the center of the barracks was a sort of hallway where we used to sit around and gab. And the walls . . . well, they were old, too. We'd come back to the place on some nights a little drunk on beer and put our fists through the walls. They weren't very solid. And then the next day we'd tape up the holes, try and hide them so we wouldn't get suspended.

The guys who lived there were real close. The first year I roomed with Jerry Bumbacco from back home in the Soo. Jerry was one of the guys who got me interested in attending Michigan Tech. We used to have a lot of fun and raise a lot of hell.

My greatest memory of that first year at college was a four-day beer-drinking binge we went on in May. It started on a Thursday night. We had just completed a tough exam period and we wanted to celebrate. We marched from bar to bar, drinking beer and playing pool and bowling on those little machines. Then at night we'd wind up back at the barracks, drinking more beer.

One of those days during that "Lost Weekend" was unusually warm for May in Houghton — maybe seventy-five degrees — so we went out to the breakwaters on Lake Superior, fifteen miles out of town. We were still going pretty good. On the way out there we picked up a few six-packs of beer and put them in the water to keep them chilled. We stayed at the beach until six or seven that night. By that time we're pretty sun-burned and really looped. We head back to Houghton and wind up in one of the bars near the college, horsing around and having fun.

One guy throws a beer in another's face and suddenly everybody is in the act and the bartender is going nuts. So we wind up throwing beer on him and he's drenched and throws us out of the place.

It finally ended on a Sunday night. I don't think I ever put away as much beer as I did during those four days and I was damn glad the hockey season was over because I was really out of shape.

I should point out here, though, that my freshman year wasn't one beer-drinking binge after another. I studied hard — well, hard enough to be an average student. And I had a better than average season playing with Tech's freshman hockey team.

It's difficult for me to recall now what my goals-allowed average was during my freshman year, but I felt I wouldn't have any trouble moving up to the varsity the next year. And I made it, too. Although Rick Best and I shared the goaltending, I was named to the All-America team in my sophomore season.

Still, I couldn't seem to avoid trouble. During those first two years I became friendly with George Hill, who lived in a room next to me at the end of the barracks. George was from Flin Flon, Manitoba. He was a real hot-scoring junior hockey player before showing up at Tech. In fact, he led the junior league out West for two or three years.

George was a tough guy, too, about five-foot-nine and one hundred sixty-five pounds. Not too big but tough. He used to like to fight, so we made a great twosome.

I was involved in one incident with George that almost got me thrown out of college. It happened during my freshman year and involved some local toughs, non-students at Houghton.

There's a lot of animosity between local people and the college. I don't know why because the college kept them going. But I guess they hated us. They sort of depended on us and I guess they resented it, or something. Especially the local guys, the uneducated guys, you know, who think they're tough guys.

Once we were at this friend's house and these local guys came over causing trouble. Our cars were parked . . . and they knew who we were, I guess, so we go out and George is talking to this guy and we're sort of in a circle. There's our guys and their guys, you know the way . . . this is at a private home and you're having a few beers and you don't want to be bucked. Then a guy bugs you and at the time . . . my first year and I'm nineteen years old . . . I'm a little hot head.

So here I was on the step and the guy's standing five feet from me and George is in between. I just pushed George and nailed the guy at the same time and caught him right in the mouth. Knocked out two of his front teeth . . . and this started a fight. Each guy paired off, and we really gave it to these guys. They were small guys looking for trouble so we gave 'em the trouble.

This guy got me mad because I hit him and he went down and as he was getting up on one knee I gave him a real kick. I guess I got him on the jaw. And as he was going down he reached and he caught my pants and he ripped them. That was what really aggravated me. And then the guy ripped my pants nearly off. Later he had the nerve to try and sue me. I think our coach got into the picture and got it straightened out somehow.

Another time we were in this Houghton bar and we left our table to talk to a friend. We came back to our table — it was a packed house — and there were three guys sitting in our seats. So we just said, "This is our table, you guys, so would you kindly move." And one guy with the other gang says, "Buzz off." They were all big guys, believe me.

George tried to reason with them.

"This is our table, you bastards," he said. "We just left it for a few minutes and you guys try to take over."

Then George belted this one guy in the mouth. Now everybody was throwing punches.

During the fight, I looked up and George was on top of one guy and another was coming to get him from behind. He was ready to clobber old George. I saw this while fighting with another guy.

I picked up a glass and tossed it at the sneaky guy and hit him in the head. It cut him wide open and now that guy was finished, bleeding all over.

They took him to the hospital and when they found glass in his head they called the cops. Oh, oh. This was serious. You know, hitting a guy with a deadly weapon or something like that. Well, the cops came to get me the next day. They wanted to see me in the dean's office.

Now I was really in trouble. They were ready to charge me

with a felony, which would have gotten me thrown out of the country. But the dean of students, Harold Meese, came to my rescue. He liked me despite the reputation I was getting as a troublemaker.

"Tony," he said, "I never like to see any student kicked out of the country," he said. "So I'm going to do all I can to help you."

"I'd really appreciate that, Mr. Meese," I said. "I like it here at Tech and I like playing hockey for the school. I certainly don't want to end up back in the Soo now."

I still don't know how Mr. Meese did it, but the charges were dropped against me. I had to pay for the cleaning bills of the guy I hit, but that's all. And I was allowed to remain in school.

Following that incident, I started to taper off, at least when it came to fighting. I was losing that chip on my shoulder. And, more important, I was becoming an important member of the hockey team.

We climaxed the 1964-65 season by winning the NCAA championship and I was named to the All-America team, quite an honor for a sophomore. Strangely, that may have been my best season in college hockey. I played pretty well in my junior year, but things started to get under my skin. It began with the fall term.

I had an average that was just a little less than a C that term because I wasn't doing enough studying. I was lazy. I don't know why. I just seemed to be lazy all the time. Anyway, I made it through that fall okay and then came the winter and hockey. That meant we started traveling all over.

We made a trip to Boston and won the Boston Arena Christmas Tournament. I played all the games there because that's when the other goalie, Rick Best, had a broken hand and I was named the tournament's Most Valuable Player.

The championship game in the tournament was a thriller. It was against Boston University. We scored four goals in the final ten minutes to win, 5–2. B.U. was leading, 2–1, when Colin Patterson scored on one of our power plays to tie the score at 10:16 of the last period.

Right then I figured we'd win, and I was right. Gary Milroy set up Wayne Weller for the tie-breaking goal, then Milroy and Fred Hall added insurance goals for us in the final two minutes.

Tony won all kinds of awards at Michigan Tech.

Our forward line of Milroy, Patterson and Weller was fantastic in that game. It accounted for four of the five goals and totaled five assists. I played a pretty good game, making thirty-five saves. Seventeen of these came in the second period, but the only one I remember was a glove save I made on Jimmy Wood of B.U. right in front of the net. A Boston writer called that "the biggest steal of the tournament," and that made me feel proud.

The pressure, though, was beginning to build up in me by now. You only play a limited number of games in college and they press you to win them all. Who likes to lose? Nobody likes to lose, I'm sure. Especially me. But the pressure of *win, win, win* gets you after a while.

Later that season, my brother Phil watched me play in the Great Lakes Invitational Tournament in Detroit. He was then with the Black Hawks and made the trip from Chicago to check me out. He must have suspected something was wrong.

After one of the games, Phil came to me and asked, "How's it going, Bomby?"

I looked at Phil and said, "Hell, I don't know. You saw me play. I figure I'm doing okay."

He gave me that old big brother pat on the back and said, "You've got to hang in there, Bomby. Give it all you've got. And keep after those books, too. You've got to get that degree."

I wasn't kidding old Phil. I was starting to lose my incentive, on the ice and in the classroom, and he realized it. I was worrying about how many credits I was carrying and whether I would graduate.

Speaking of Phil, a few times while I was at school I got some of the gang together and we'd drive down to Chicago to watch him play for the Black Hawks. And every time we'd show up in Chicago Stadium he'd stink out the place. I never saw him play a good game in those days.

Phil wasn't the only member of the Hawks who was being booed by the Stadium fans then. There was one game I saw — I don't recall who the Hawks were playing — but Glenn Hall, who was then their goalie, let in a terrible goal. It was a real beauty, just like I miss sometimes with the Hawks.

It was a shot from the blue line and it trickled through Hall's legs. Hall was embarrassed, naturally, and the fans . . . did they get on him. Chicago fans are demanding. I knew how Glenn felt that night. I've since learned how a guy can be nervous in front of twenty thousand fans . . . good fans but avid fans. It's really tough sometimes playing in Chicago Stadium.

The summer between my junior and senior years I decided to remain in Houghton so I could attend summer school. I took a couple or three courses and this helped ease my mind. What the hell, you get a free ride for four years and then after the ride is over you have to pay the piper or you don't graduate. And I wanted that degree.

When summer school was over, I went home and took the big step: I married Marilyn Mezzone. Marilyn and I had dated while in high school and we got engaged during my second year at Michigan Tech. It was quite a wedding. Phil was my best man and his wife, Linda, was a bridesmaid.

We honeymooned at a fishing camp in the Green Bay, Wisconsin, area and then it was time to return to school. Marilyn gave up her job in a bank in the Soo and we moved into the married students' housing development at school.

Marriage must have agreed with me because my grades started to rise again in my senior year. I spent more time at the books and I averaged better than a B-minus, which was damn good for me. I also played well enough to make the All-America hockey team for the third straight year, and that's not bad either.

I'd be completely dishonest, though, if I didn't admit I had a little trouble adjusting to married life. It was tough on Marilyn, too, and it must have been lonely for her at times. She had never been away from home before.

I used to study until about eleven at night and then go out and have a few beers with the guys. I'd come home around one-thirty or two in the morning. That was the life I had become used to and it was hard to change. It was also a little rugged having somebody tell me what to do with my free time. But we eventually made the adjustment.

Adjusting to the classroom, however, was tougher. One of the toughest teachers I encountered at Tech was a man named Jack Remington. He taught economics. We used to call him "Smiling

Jack" because that's all he did was smile. But he was tough. He'd say, "Hey, this is a tough test," and he'd smile.

He also used to proctor exams. He'd walk down the aisle in soft shoes and used to pride himself on catching students cheating. I found out how tough he was to fool once while taking one of his exams.

Before I went into his class I was worried as hell because I knew it would be rough. One of the older guys told me "Smiling Jack" didn't see too well through his thick eyeglasses. "If you get stuck," the guy said, "try an eyeball." In other words, glance quickly at somebody else's paper and try to pick up a couple of points.

So I went in for the exam and there was old "Smiling Jack." Smiling, of course. Right off the bat, I'm stuck for a couple of answers. I just couldn't concentrate, so I decide to do a little peeking. I figured "Smiling Jack" isn't going to be watching that closely.

While he's walking down the aisle, away from me, I raised myself up a little, stretched, and glanced at another guy's paper. As I'm stretching, "Smiling Jack" spins around and catches me in the act. I sat down and he confronted me.

"Mr. Esposito," he said, "I do believe you're trying to cheat on this exam."

"No, sir," I said, "you're mistaken. I was just stretching my legs." What else could I say? I had to deny it. I'd still deny it today if he asked me.

The other thing I can't deny about my days at Tech is that coach John MacInnes and I never really got along very well. I performed for him, I did the best I could in every game, but there was friction.

I remember one incident during my final year at Tech. We had just finished a big set of exams. One afternoon before practice, three or four of us stopped in for a beer. We had more than a few and by the time we got to the rink for practice we were hammered. A couple of the guys were falling all over the ice. They couldn't stand up.

I could hold my beer a little better than the others, so I got out on the ice and had no trouble. I had a good practice . . . one of my better practices, in fact.

Then a little trouble brewed. Bill Lucier, the assistant coach, had been watching me and at the end of practice he went to MacInnes.

"I can smell beer on Tony," he told MacInnes.

"Aw, he probably had a couple," Coach said. "He just finished exams, you know, and got a little thirsty."

Lucier shook his head. "He had more than a couple," he said. "I could smell the beer coming through his pores all through practice. He must have had more than a gallon."

That was all MacInnes had to hear. He suspended me from the team. And though he later lifted the suspension, this really teed me off.

I never agreed with Coach's philosophy anyway. He was a good coach, but I didn't like the way he treated his players. He treated us like we were kids. I was then twenty-two years old and you don't treat a player like a kid at twenty-two. Hell, I wanted a few beers. If there was a game I'd never touch the stuff, but this was before a practice and we'd just finished a crucial exam and I felt like relaxing.

College, I feel, is not so much that you're crammed with knowledge; it's learning how to get along in this world. And that's what I learned — how to handle people and how to deal with people.

Of course, it also helps to study and keep your grades up and get that degree. I never was a brain. I never claimed to be. Still, I finished college with a C-plus average and ranked two hundred fiftieth in our graduating class of some six hundred.

I emerged from Michigan Tech with a Bachelor of Science degree in business administration and a desire to play pro hockey.

Now I felt I was ready to face the world and match my education against the old-school business dealings of Sam Pollock, the general manager of the Montreal Canadiens.

CHAPTER X

CHOKE

*In the spring of 1967 Phil Esposito suffered
through two memorable experiences. One was pain-
fully humorous, the other was just painful.*

The Black Hawks were flying high when the 1967 Stanley Cup
playoffs rolled around. This would be the final playoffs before
expansion and we wanted to become the last champions of the old
six-team league.

We concluded our regular season by bombing the Rangers, 8–0,
at New York. Four nights later we faced the Toronto Maple Leafs
in the first game of the opening round at the Chicago Stadium.
The Maple Leafs had finished third, nineteen points behind the
Hawks. We figured to sweep them in four straight.

The embarrassment I suffered in that series will live with me
for the rest of my life. It started in the opening game. I got into
a fight with Tim Horton. He picked me up — God, he was strong —
and a skate got caught in my pants and ripped them open. I didn't
realize what had happened until after the fight when I felt this
draft around my crotch. Then I looked into the stands and it seemed
like all eighteen thousand fans in Chicago Stadium were laughing
at me and my predicament. Bobby Hull skated up to me and said,
"Don't look now, pal, but your jock is hanging out."

Have you ever seen those clowns in an ice show run on their
skates? That's how I must have looked. I didn't skate to the penalty
box, I ran. The officials then let me go to our locker room downstairs and put on another pair of pants. When I got back, the fans
were still giggling.

We won the opener, 5–2, so that helped me forget the ripped

79

pants episode. But what followed was far more embarrassing to me and the entire Chicago team. Terry Sawchuk was completing his last season as the Leafs' goalie and he was magnificent. We won only one of the next five games and were eliminated. Terry and Johnny Bower then teamed up to help Toronto beat Montreal in the final series.

I failed to score a single point in the six-game series against Toronto. The previous season I had only one goal in six playoff games. So now the Chicago fans and the writers were really on me. I remember Dan Moulton writing, "Well, Espo failed in the playoffs again."

Chico Maki and Doug Mohns, Red Hay and Dennis Hull and Ken Hodge didn't score a goal in that 1967 playoff either. But I was the scapegoat. Espo failed again. You shove that stuff down a person's throat long enough and he's going to start thinking about it and he's going to be dead.

In my case, I was already dead — at least as far as the Black Hawks' management was concerned. Tommy Ivan and Billy Reay had me on the trading block before I could pack my equipment at the end of the playoffs.

I remember walking into Ivan's office and asking for expense money for my trip home. He wouldn't even talk to me. He yelled at his secretary, "Get that guy out of here. I don't want to see him. Get him out."

Ivan got rid of me for good a month later. It was May 15, 1967. That was the date when the six established teams were forced to "freeze" their rosters for the first expansion draft at Montreal in June. The Black Hawks beat the deadline by five minutes.

I was attending a reception for a sports celebrity banquet in the Soo. It was held at the home of a friend, Russ Ramsey. Johnny Bower was there and Roger Crozier and Matt Ravlich. Crozier, who was then with the Red Wings, kept bugging me about rumors he had heard concerning me.

"You're coming to Detroit, Phil," Crozier kept whispering in my ear. "I got the word the other day. You're going to be playing for us next season."

It was about five minutes before midnight when the telephone rang. Russ answered it. "It's for you, Phil," he said. "It's your wife."

I left the gang and took the call on an upstairs phone. It was Linda all right.

"Phil," she said, "you've just been traded to Boston."

"Boston?" I shouted. "Oh, God, Linda, I can't believe it. You've gotta be kidding me."

"I'm not kidding."

"Who else is involved? Is it a big deal?"

"A real big one," Linda said. "Six players. The Bruins are sending Pit Martin, Gilles Marotte and Jack Norris to Chicago for you, Ken Hodge and Fred Stanfield."

"Hodgie, too. And Freddy. Oh, my God. Wait till they get the news. Boston? Linda, I still can't believe it. I'll be home in an hour."

When I walked back downstairs my face must have been as white as a ghost. Everybody was looking at me and asking, "What happened, Phil? Is it bad news?"

"Bad enough," I said. "I've been traded to Boston."

Now it was their turn to be shocked.

"Boston?" Ravlich said. "I can't believe it."

Crozier said, "I would have bet you were coming to Detroit, Phil."

Then they joined together and kept repeating things like, "You'll really like it there, Phil," and "Boston's not a bad hockey town, you know." They could see I was down in the dumps and were trying to build up my spirits.

I got back on the phone and made a few calls. First, I called the radio-TV station (CJIC) where I had a sports show and was able to announce my own trade over the air. Then I called my two closest friends on the Black Hawks — Bobby Hull and Chico Maki.

Bobby thought I had been drinking and was pulling his leg. "Don't go away," he said. "I'll call you right back." I figured he put through a call to Chicago, got the trade verified, and then phoned me.

"Phil," he said, "you weren't kidding. Those no-good, stupid bastards in Chicago have really unloaded you. It's incredible, but they've done it."

"I know, I know, Bobby. What am I going to do about it?"

"The only thing you can do, Phil, is to accept it. Go to Boston, play good hockey and show those jerks what a mistake they made."

Chico Maki offered me the same advice that night. "You're just going to have to work your ass off for the Bruins," he said. "Do that and you'll find your own reward."

I was able to joke about the trade later with Bobby and Chico, but deep down I was hurt and sorry to break up our partnership. We had been real close buddies. Still, in this business you make new friends quickly, and I did in Boston, believe me.

The first thing I had to swallow was my pride. I was moving from a first-place team that had been in the playoffs for nine straight years to a team that had finished last six times in the past seven seasons.

But I figured the trade provided me with one major opportunity — to make more money. The Bruins didn't have a superstar at the time. Bobby Orr was destined to be, but he had just completed his rookie season, so the Bruins didn't have a real high-salaried player on their roster.

The Hawks had too many All-Star salaries during my four years with the club to pay me what I thought I was worth. I had a base pay of seventy-five hundred as a rookie, jumped to twelve thousand in my second year and to thirteen thousand the following year. My base pay for my fourth and final season with the Hawks was seventeen-five.

The first thing the Bruins did after I joined the club was to boost my salary to twenty-two thousand. I considered it a vote of confidence and really appreciated it. I also felt good when they made me an assistant captain soon after I showed up at their training camp in London, Ontario.

Only one thing disturbed me when I got my first look at the Boston club. Most of the guys had a losing complex, even in camp. You could see it and feel it. They had been losers for many years and I had never played with losers. Chicago had always made the playoffs while I was there, and this was important to me.

I remember sitting in a bar in London after one training camp session. A bunch of the players were there, sipping beer and talking about the new season ahead. Some of the born losers on the team — I don't want to mention any names but they were mainly veterans — were saying, "Well, let's get this season over with in a hurry . . . it won't be any different than the past seasons."

This kind of talk really teed me off, so I spoke up. I had a few beers in me and sometimes I get brave when I'm drinking.

"Look," I said, "if there's one sonofagun here who doesn't want to win now and doesn't want to win this season there's no need for him to be on this team. Some of you guys are going to hate me after this season is over, but I'm telling you we're going to win. "If we don't win it will be the fault of guys who are quitters. I never was a quitter in my life and I don't like to play with a quitter."

Teddy Green, who was my roomie at that training camp, really liked that little speech. He came back to our room and said, "Phil, it was great. That's what some of the guys needed. And I'm with you. Just watch, we'll make the playoffs this season."

Derek Sanderson was breaking in with the Bruins and I liked the kid. But would you believe he then had an inferiority complex? About his playing ability I mean. Derek and Don Awrey shared an adjoining room and Derek used to come to me for advice.

"Phil," he'd say, "I'm worried. I don't know if I can make this club."

"Don't worry so much," I'd tell him. "You can't miss. Just keep working."

If Derek thanked me once he thanked me a thousand times later for keeping him going in training camp. And he made the team before we left camp and headed for Boston, where we opened the 1967-68 season against the Detroit Red Wings.

It was a little strange sitting in the Bruins' dressing room before our opener in Boston Garden. Except for Hodge and Stanfield, I was still among strangers. Kenny, Freddy and I had known what it was to be with a winner and, damn, we wanted to instill that winning spirit in the others.

The attitude among the Bruins before the game was good. It got even better when John Bucyk scored for us in the first period, beating Roger Crozier, the guy who had predicted I would wind up with Detroit. Stanfield drew an assist on Bucyk's goal, then Hodge set up a goal by Tommy Williams early in the second period to give us a 2–0 lead. Freddy and Kenny were instant heroes with the Boston fans.

The Red Wings, though, scored three consecutive goals later

In his new uniform Phil figured he had to try harder.

in the second period, which ended in a 3–3 tie. When Bucyk set up a goal by John McKenzie with two minutes gone in the third period, I figured we had it in the bag. We all started to work like hell to protect that one-goal lead for Gerry Cheevers.

But with three minutes left to play, Dallas Smith was penalized for hooking. Gordie Howe came out to lead the Detroit power play and set up Dean Prentice for the tying goal with time running out. That's the way it ended. A 4–4 tie. For the Bruins, it was a moral victory.

Our next game was against the Montreal Canadiens at Boston Garden. I remember going to the rink that night with Ron Murphy. It was a miserable night and I felt awful. I had a cold and a blasted headache. While we were dressing before the game I knew if we were going to show the Boston fans we weren't born losers, this would be the night to prove it. The Canadiens were the haughty, snooty kingpins of the league, despite their loss to Toronto in the Stanley Cup finals the previous spring.

Some of the fans in the sellout crowd of 13,909 weren't even seated when I batted in Stanfield's off-balance centering pass after only thirty-four seconds. My first goal as a Bruin. Geez, I forgot all about my head cold.

Tommy Williams set me up for two more goals during a twenty-seven-second span later in the opening period and the Boston fans went nuts. So did I. When Rogie Vachon, the Montreal goalie, flipped the puck out of the net after my third goal, I grabbed it as a souvenir. It was my first hat trick in the NHL.

Late in the second period, I worked my way in front of Vachon and rapped in a pass from Bucyk for my fourth straight goal. That gave me a super hat trick and the Bruins a 6–2 victory.

It was a big night for me and a big night for the Bruins. But the thing I remember was the scene in our dressing room after the game. The guys were patting me on the back and kidding around and then somebody, I can't recall who it was, said, "Hey, with a guy as lucky as Phil around, maybe we'll have a winning team this season."

That remark pleased me more than my four goals. Honest. The Bruins were starting to find out that they weren't born losers after all.

We went on from there to lose only five of our first twenty-two games and were leading the East Division. I had ten goals by then, but none against the Black Hawks when they came into Boston Garden for a game on December 2. Denis DeJordy shut me out again as we battled the Hawks to a 4–4 tie. That was a game in which Bobby Hull and I barely escaped serious injury.

Bobby had a partial breakaway in the second period. I was chasing him from behind and my stick got caught and he went flying into the net and I went crashing into the backboards. Linda was at the game. She jumped up and saw Bobby lying on the ice. She turned to a friend and said, "Gee, I hope Bobby didn't get hurt." Nice wife. There I was lying on the ice, too, behind the net, but she couldn't see me.

Bobby got up first, skated over to his old buddy and said, "Cripes, Phil, you want to get us both killed?"

I apologized and said, "Bob, I don't know what the hell happened, but I went down pretty hard too." Then we both started laughing, maybe because we were happy to be alive.

There are times when I do a lot of talking on the ice, even to guys from the other team if they're old friends. I don't believe in that crap you shouldn't talk to your rivals. I always try just as hard to beat those guys I gab with. Some players, I know, feel differently about this. I respect their opinions and feelings and hope they respect mine.

The Black Hawks were back in Boston during Christmas week, and by now I was aching to score against my old teammates. Before the game I kidded around with both Hull and Chico Maki, but I think they knew I was uptight. Frankly, I was tight as a drum.

I finally loosened up after beating DeJordy about midway through the first period. When I got back to the bench I was tempted to thumb my nose at Billy Reay, but that would have been bush. So I just grinned at him and the rest of the Chicago team. I got another goal before the end of the period and added another in the second to complete my second hat trick.

After one of those goals, Tommy Williams skated by Hull and said, "Hey, Bobby, thanks for giving us Esposito. He's a helluva hockey player." Bobby waited until Williams skated close to him again and whispered, "I wish we still had Phil."

We used that 7–2 victory to snap Chicago's ten-game winning streak and tie the Black Hawks for first place. I went to Harry Sinden, our coach, after the game and told him we'd make the playoffs for sure. We had captured that winning spirit. Our guys were playing well, we wanted to win as a team, and nobody was backing off.

Then we ran into some tough injuries. Orr, who had suffered a cracked collarbone in December and banged up a shoulder in the All-Star Game in January, needed surgery for removal of cartilage in his left knee. Bobby went into the hospital on February 12, the same day Linda gave birth to our second daughter, Carrie.

I had taken Linda to the hospital two days before the Bruins were to leave on a sixteen-day road trip. She was induced and Carrie was born the next day. By the time I got back to Boston, little Carrie looked like she had grown fifteen feet.

During that road trip I was having trouble with badly stretched ligaments in my right knee. I was examined by the Seals' team doctor in Oakland and he said I'd be lucky to finish the season. But I continued to play after being fitted with a brace and eventually the trouble cleared up.

By the time March rolled around, Montreal had opened a healthy first-place lead while we were battling the Hawks and the Rangers for second. And I mean battle. One of our best scrappers that season was Eddie Shack. He got into a brutal fight with Larry Zeidel, who was with Philadelphia. Zeidel started it by cross-checking Shack as he skated across the Philly blue line. They then started swinging their sticks like axes. When they finally stopped, blood was flowing down Zeidel's face and Shack had little cuts all over his head and face. Both players were suspended, Zeidel for four games and Shack for three.

I also got into a late-season battle with Stan Mikita — but this one involved points, not sticks. Going into the final night of the regular season, Stan led me by a single point for the league scoring championship. We played the Maple Leafs at Boston Garden and the Hawks, starting an hour later, faced the Red Wings at Chicago.

I had to settle for a single goal against Toronto while Mikita got a goal and two assists to win his fourth scoring title in five years. Punch Imlach, who was coaching Toronto, pulled a dirty trick on me that night. He assigned Bob Pulford to me and told him if he let me get so much as one point Punch would fire him. Pulford told me that himself.

At one point in the game, I turned to Pulford and said: "Hey, Bob, what are you doing to me? You guys aren't making the playoffs so this game means nothing to you. Why not let me go and play my own game?"

Pulford said, "I'm sorry about that, Phil, but I've got a job to do. Punch told me to stay with you and don't worry about scoring, just so you don't score. If I don't obey him I'm going to be fired. What can I do?"

I've always liked Bob and I understood his predicament. He did one helluva checking job on me that night. But that damn Imlach. He really burned me up. Near the end of the game I skated by the Toronto bench and hollered, "Punch, you're a baldheaded bastard," then added a few more choice words for good measure.

The disappointment I felt over losing the scoring title was minor compared to the fate I suffered in the 1968 Stanley Cup playoffs. I had scored thirty-five goals during the regular season and led the league in assists with forty-nine to help the Bruins into the playoffs for the first time in nine years. But the Canadiens eliminated us in four games and all I accounted for were three assists.

Gump Worsley played fantastic against us. I had always found him to be the toughest goalie in the league to score on and this time he stopped me cold. Actually, none of us played too well. We were all jittery and nervous.

It was Chicago all over again for me . . . especially the newspapers claiming Phil Esposito choked in the playoffs. It was getting so bad that I was starting to believe those "choke" stories, too.

CHAPTER XI

"YOU'LL MAKE IT TONY"

His All-America college days behind him, Tony
Esposito had but one desire — to become the second
member of his family to star in the National Hockey
League. But he didn't make the big jump overnight.

Following my first varsity season at Michigan Tech I learned
I had been placed on the Montreal Canadiens' negotiation list.
That gave them the right to negotiate for my services if I intended
to turn pro.

No other pro club could approach me, and I feel this is a part
of pro hockey's structure that is deplorable.

What right did the Canadiens have to place me on their list
in the first place? I was an independent player, or so I thought. I
had never had any affiliation with Montreal, but now they were
telling me if I wanted to turn pro it would have to be with them
and on their terms.

Under these conditions, a young player is just a pawn in the
hands of management. You're strapped. You have nowhere to go.
You just sit tight and if they make you an offer and you find it
unacceptable, you can't do a damn thing about it.

In my case, the Canadiens had one of their scouts, Mickey
Hennessey, keeping tabs on me while I was at Michigan Tech.
He would drift in and watch our games and drift out. I never
talked to him personally until my final year at college.

In the summer of 1967, the year I graduated, Hennessey visited
me in the Soo and offered me a contract. It was a lousy offer and
I turned it down. It was for something like seven thousand a season
. . . real chicken feed. We spent most of the summer bickering over

the contract, then just before the Canadiens went to training camp I talked to Sam Pollock, their general manager.

Pollock increased the offer to twelve thousand . . . a two thousand dollar bonus and a ten thousand dollar minor league contract. I still wasn't satisfied.

"There's no way I'm going to play for that kind of money," I told Pollock.

"Well," he said, "you can take it or leave it. That's my final offer."

"Okay," I said, "I'll leave it. Your offer is a joke."

Actually, I really wanted to play. Up to this point in my life I was always being referred to as "that other Esposito, Phil's kid brother," and I guess it sort of irritated me. I wanted to prove I could make it in the big leagues, too.

I then got another phone call from Pollock. We discussed the contract, but I was still dissatisfied. However, I was getting itchy to play by now.

"How about my coming to camp, Mr. Pollock, and we can continue our discussions there?" I said. "I'd like to get on the ice and show you what I can do. If you think I'm worth more money then, well, you can pay it. If you don't think so, you can tell me and I'll get lost."

He finally agreed to that proposal, so I packed my bag and reported to the Canadiens' Cleveland farm club in Sherbrooke. Fred Glover was the Cleveland coach and I think he liked my style. But I was still having my troubles with Pollock.

The day before the end of training camp, Pollock called me in for another contract talk. I told him I wanted at least fifteen thousand to start, then if I found I was wasting my time I would bail out after a year or two. I knew I was going to be in the minors first because I needed experience. I figured it would take me maybe two years to make the National League. If I didn't make it by then, I would quit.

Pollock was a little more receptive by now and we worked out a pretty decent bonus deal. I was promised bonuses for shutouts and for maintaining a certain goals average. Another clause involved the team standings. If our team finished first I would get an extra thousand or if it wound up second I'd get seven hundred fifty.

When we totaled it all up I was guaranteed about eighteen

thousand if I had a good season. That was more like it. What the heck, eighteen thousand for playing in the minors is pretty good dough. So Sam and I shook on it and I was assigned to Cleveland at the start of the 1967-68 season.

Gerry Desjardins, now a teammate on the Black Hawks, was Cleveland's number one goalie when I joined the club. He had played the previous two seasons with Houston of the Central League. In those days, Gerry was a little erratic and I think my presence helped him get rolling.

In practice and in exhibition games, Gerry wasn't really putting out or giving it one hundred per cent. Then I started to put a little pressure on him. I pushed him pretty good because I was having a good training camp and as a result he started to work harder.

Eventually, Gerry developed into a damn good goalie. His style is similar to mine. And he's very agile, especially for such a big man. He's over two hundred pounds, but he's solid and he can really move around in front of the net.

I was happy when the Hawks got Gerry from Los Angeles in the 1969-70 season. He keeps me on my toes and forces me to play a little better, just as I did for him in 1967, pushing him so he got in top shape.

Gerry, in fact, played so well at the start of that season — I think he won seven or eight straight games for Cleveland — I couldn't break into the Barons' lineup. So before I got the chance to play a single game for Cleveland, Pollock arranged to loan me to Vancouver, which was then in the Western League, so I could get some experience.

It didn't take me long to break into the Vancouver lineup. I joined the club in Rochester, N.Y., and made my pro debut on November 4, 1967, against the Rochester Americans. I was a little shaky but so were my new teammates, who had lost their last eight games.

The coach of the Vancouver club was Jim Gregory, who later became general manager of the Toronto Maple Leafs. He could see how nervous I was and said, "Tony, just go out there and do the best you can. Don't worry about a thing."

But I was really worried. I didn't know whether I could play in the pros or not. Aside from exhibition games, I never had had real pros firing .the puck at me. I wondered what it would be like. I found out soon enough. In the first period, Milan Marcetta beat me with a shot that I should have stopped. I was down on the ice and he jammed it underneath me. What a coincidence that was, having Marcetta score the first goal off me. I had remembered him from the Soo where he once played center for the Soo Thunderbirds.

I fanned on two other shots that night — I can't remember who shot them — and the game wound up in a 3–3 tie. Not bad for a pro debut, I thought. Gregory was just as pleased as I to pick up a point, the club's first in nine games.

We headed back home to Vancouver and about two or three weeks later I had my wife join me. She was pregnant at the time. Both of us loved Vancouver. It's a picturesque, beautiful city.

Vancouver looked even more beautiful to me after I got my first shutout as a pro there. I'll never forget the date. It was November 21, 1967, and it was a 5–0 whitewash job against San Diego. I almost lost the shutout in the final minute when Willie O'Ree — he used to play for the Boston Bruins — caught me out of position. But Larry McNabb, one of our defensemen at Vancouver, came out of nowhere to block O'Ree's shot.

In my next game, three nights later at Vancouver, I blanked Seattle by the same 5–0 score. Two straight shutouts! Wow! I figured Sam Pollock would read that in the papers and tell me to catch the next plane to Montreal.

Any thoughts I had of making that jump into the NHL were shattered a few weeks later in a game at San Diego. I was pulled out of the game late in the second period after giving up six goals. San Diego then got six more goals against my replacement, Jean Guy Morissette, to win, 12–2.

I felt sick after the game. Actually, I didn't give up any real bad goals, but it was just one of those nights when everything went against me. The puck would hit one of our guys or a stick and bounce into the net.

When Gregory yanked me I wasn't mad at him, just mad at myself for letting in those six goals. He came to me later and said, "Forget it, Tony. It wasn't your fault. It was strictly a team effort. Everybody was plain lousy."

I tried to shrug it off, but I was worried. It took me two or three games to get back on the track. I was young — only twenty-three — and I figured the balloon had burst and I had ruined my chances of making it in the NHL.

Shortly after mid-season our team moved into the Pacific Coliseum. We had been playing in the Vancouver Forum, which was like an old barn. It was cold and the lighting was bad but most of the older players liked it.

I still feel one of the reasons we didn't make the Western League playoffs that season was because we couldn't adjust to the new Coliseum. You don't have to be in as good shape to play in a cold rink as you do in a warm one. Some of our guys weren't in shape, so the heat and the larger rink affected them.

I also had a little trouble over the last half of that rookie season. I was handling an average of forty shots a game. I didn't mind that but I found I just couldn't take it over a long haul like I thought I could. It was getting to me, all that pressure, and I found myself becoming irritable.

With the Black Hawks I've found that some nights I don't feel just right, but the team senses this and helps carry the load. It was different with Vancouver. I knew I had to be really on the ball, but there were some games when I didn't have it. Then I'd give up five or six goals and want to fight everybody.

I did have some pretty good fights in that league, too. I took on Guyle Fielder one night. He was the perennial scoring champion in the Western League. In this particular game he tripped me in the crease after taking a shot. I got up mad as hell and jumped him. That was a good one.

Another time I got a ten-minute misconduct penalty and a fine for fighting. That's when I started to wise up. I decided I was being a sucker giving away my money to the league instead of keeping it in my pocket. Also, once you blow your cool you get back in the net and you're still steaming and have trouble concentrating on your job. I leave the fighting now to the defensemen. That's what they get paid for, protecting me.

The Vancouver team that season wasn't too bad, but we just couldn't seem to jell. We had some young guys like Terry Clancy and Bob Lemieux, Mike Corbett and Ron Boehm, Tracy Pratt and

Larry Mavety. Also, some oldtimers like Billy McNeill and Gerry Odrowski, Phil Maloney and Larry Popein.

Popein, who once played for the New York Rangers and later became a coach in their organization, was from the old school, a tough man to fathom. He would sit in the dressing room and mind his own business and never say anything. If you talked to him, he'd tell you how much tougher it was when he joined the pros, but that's all he'd ever talk about. Old guys don't tell the young kids anything that would help them.

So we younger guys struggled along at Vancouver, making mistakes like all young guys do, but learning from these mistakes, too.

Two weeks before the end of the season — around mid-March — my wife, Marilyn, flew back home to the Soo. She was then seven and one-half months pregnant and wanted to be near her parents when our child was born.

I didn't play too well during the tailend of the season. I guess I was lonesome for Marilyn and I was a little worried about her condition. Anyway, we lost four of our last five games and failed to make the playoffs.

The season ended on a Friday night, March 29. I stayed around Vancouver a day or two to clean up some business and then flew home. The next day — April 4 — Marilyn gave birth to a fine, bouncing boy. We named him Mark Anthony. He was a little premature — being born about a month early — but a wonderful, healthy baby.

I was as jittery as any expectant father sweating out his first child that day at the hospital. But I had another reason to be a little anxious. Phil was playing for the Bruins against the Canadiens at eight that night in the Stanley Cup playoffs and I wanted to watch the game on television.

Marilyn proved to be very cooperative. She gave birth at seven-thirty. I rushed home and got there five minutes before the start of the game. The Bruins lost and were swept out of the playoffs in four games. Poor Phil didn't score a single goal.

Phil came home a few days later and we discussed my future. I had completed that first pro year at Vancouver with four shutouts and an average of 3.20 goals allowed per game. Not bad, although I thought my average could have been better.

I had only one thought in mind and I told Phil about it. "I want to make the NHL, but I don't want to kick around in the minors for years, waiting for that chance. I'm going to give myself one more year down there. Then if I don't make it, I'll quit."

Phil listened quietly and said, "You'll make it Tony, maybe in less than a year."

CHAPTER XII

UNHAPPY DEBUT

With one year of pro hockey behind him Tony Esposito figured he was ready for the National Hockey League. But first he had to employ some of the lessons he learned in his business administration courses in college at contract signing time.

The name of the game is money. It is for me anyway. I have always felt a good day's work is worth a good day's pay. But there are some people operating teams in the National Hockey League who feel otherwise. They're making a good buck — most of them, that is — but they're not always willing to pay their help a decent salary.

When I reported to the Montreal Canadiens' training camp for the 1968-69 season I ran into the same old problem — money. They had paid me pretty well for my first pro season at Vancouver and now I wanted more dollars. Why not? The Canadiens had won the Stanley Cup for the third time in four years the previous spring. They were rich champions and I figured they should spread that wealth among their players — and that included struggling farm-hands like Tony Esposito.

I was now a man with responsibilities. Those hell-raising, beer-drinking college days were behind me. I had a wife and an infant son — two dependents — and I wasn't about to let the Canadiens short-change me.

During the summer I had worked hard at a hockey clinic in the Soo with Phil, Matt Ravlich, Gene Ubriaco and Matt Pavelich. I was in great shape when I showed up in training camp.

The other goalies in camp were Rogie Vachon, Gump Worsley,

Ernie Wakely and Phil Myre. I don't think any of them worked as hard as I did during the first few days of workouts. I had three or four shutouts in camp scrimmages and this made me feel good because I was working hard to impress Claude Ruel, who had taken over as the Canadiens' coach for retired Toe Blake.

Ruel, though, wasn't too impressed with me. He was the new man on the job, the Canadiens had won the Cup again and when you win you don't make too many changes. Ruel decided to stand pat with Worsley and Vachon as his goalies. So even though I was having a great training camp, I was told to report with Myre to Sherbrooke, Quebec, where the Houston Apollos were working out. They were operating in the Central League then and were considered the Canadiens' top farm club.

I continued to play well at Houston's camp. However, I was still unhappy because I hadn't signed a contract. I was still fighting with the Canadiens over money.

This is when Sam Pollock entered the picture — again. Like the previous year, we kept haggling over the terms of my contract. When Worsley suffered an injury in the Montreal camp, Sam really applied the pressure.

"Sign this contract," Sam said, "and with Gump hurt we'll call you up and give you a chance to play some exhibition games with the Canadiens."

It was a bad contract. I think the basic figure was about twelve thousand five hundred, with two thousand dollars in bonus money thrown in. I turned it down.

"I want the right amount of money if you want me to play for the Canadiens," I told Pollock. "If I don't get it I'm going home."

Pollock wouldn't budge. Myre went back to Montreal instead of me to serve as a backup man in the exhibition games. When Worsley shook off his injury, Myre returned to the Houston camp. I was still fighting over my contract and was ready to head back to the Soo when Pollock finally made me a decent offer.

We worked out two deals — one covering a minor-league contract for Houston and the other a major-league contract for Montreal. The bonus money amounted to about six thousand and I was guaranteed another four thousand if I was called up by the Canadiens.

I was reasonably happy when we finally broke camp and headed for Houston for the season opener against Fort Worth on October 12. I wasn't happy, though, about the weather. It was hot as hell, so I left my wife and son at home, telling Marilyn she could join me when the weather turned cooler.

Al MacNeil, who later succeeded Ruel as the Canadiens' coach, was the Apollos' player-coach. He picked me over Myre to start the opener and we beat Forth Worth, 2–1.

We had some damn good players on that Houston club. There were young guys like Christian Bordeleau and Jude Drouin, Paul Curtis and Guy Lapointe, Ernie Hicke and Lu Grenier. Among the experienced players were Al (Boom Boom) Caron, who had played with my brother when Phil was breaking into the pros at St. Louis, and MacNeil, a wily old NHL defenseman who knew all the tricks of the trade.

With Phil Myre and me alternating in goal, we lost only one of our first eleven games. I won my first five starts before losing to Kansas City, 2–1. My next start came against Dallas, a Chicago Black Hawks' farm team. It was played on our home ice in the Sam Houston Coliseum and sitting in the stands was Toe Blake, who after stepping down as the Canadiens' coach had become an assistant vice president in charge of player personnel.

I figured Blake was there to scout me and Myre because the Canadiens' goaltenders, Vachon and Worsley, weren't playing too well. I was a little nervous at the start, knowing Blake was watching, but I felt better when Bordeleau broke a scoreless tie early in the second period. Chris converted a pass from Ron Roberts by slipping the puck between the pads of Denis DeJordy, playing goal for Dallas.

Near mid-period, Garth Rizzuto of Dallas flipped a shot at me from the right corner. I was ready to block it when it hit a skate of one of our players, changed direction and bounced into the net. "That lucky bugger," I mumbled under my mask.

But Ernie Hicke and Brian Lavender scored for the Apollos before the end of the period, giving me a two-goal lead to work with. Wayne Maki, my old teammate when we played minor hockey back in the Soo, beat me in the third period. I wasn't too happy about that, either, but I settled down quickly and we wound up beating Dallas, 4–2.

Blake turned in a nice report on me when he got back to Montreal. A week later, Pollock telephoned MacNeil and told him he needed help in a hurry. By this time I had played in eight games, lost only one and had allowed only fifteen goals for a 1.80 average.

"Who is playing better, Esposito or Myre?" Pollock asked MacNeil. Hell, Sam already knew. He had Blake's report on his desk, but I guess he had to make it official.

MacNeil said, "I'd have to say Tony looks like your best bet right now, Sam."

"Okay," Sam said, "we're going to bring him up to the Canadiens. Tell Tony to get his bags packed and report to Ruel in Los Angeles."

This was my first big break and I owed it in an indirect sort of way to old Gump Worsley. He had jumped the Canadiens on a trip to the West Coast. The club had started its journey with a rough plane flight from Montreal to Chicago. Worsley, who never enjoyed flying, got off the plane in Chicago and returned to his Montreal home by train. He was on the verge of a nervous breakdown — an occupational hazard among goalies. The Canadiens, uncertain when Worsley would be mentally fit to rejoin the team, announced the following day they were bringing me up from Houston to serve as their backup goalie.

This was Tuesday, November 26, 1968. I said goodbye to my wife — she had arrived in Houston with Mark earlier that month — and caught a plane for Los Angeles. On the plane one thought kept rushing through my mind: Phil's prophesy was about to come true. He had told me that summer that I would make it to the Canadiens — maybe in less than a year. Old Phil was right again.

I can't remember if Phil phoned to congratulate me on my promotion. Probably not, because I believe the Bruins were on the road then, too.

The following night the Canadiens played the Los Angeles Kings at the Forum in Inglewood and I climbed into a Montreal uniform for the first time. What a thrill that was.

I sat on the bench and watched Vachon beat the Kings, 4–2. I thanked God that Ruel didn't call on me that night. I was as excited as hell and needed a little time to adjust to the club and the fact that I was suddenly in the National Hockey League.

Most of the Montreal players treated me fine. Mickey Redmond and Dickie Duff, who are no longer with the club, were real gentlemen. So was little Henri Richard, another nice guy.

We went out after the Los Angeles game for a few beers, then checked back into the hotel. We were to leave the following morning for Oakland. I was tired as hell because of all the traveling and excitement. I overslept the next morning and missed the team bus to the airport.

What a way for me to break in with my first NHL club. I knew if I didn't make that plane to Oakland, Claude Ruel would fine me or maybe even ship me back to Houston.

After dressing fast, I hailed a cab and headed for the airport. I didn't even know what airline the Canadiens were traveling on, and that the Los Angeles airport is huge. I kept dashing from one airline to another and finally located the team. I had made it on time.

I sort of sauntered up to the players. Ruel was there and never said a word. Whew! He either was unaware that I had overslept or he just decided to overlook it.

The temperature was seventy-five degrees when we arrived in Oakland. Beautiful weather. I did a little sightseeing, got to bed early and the following night — Friday, November 29 — we played the Seals at the Oakland Coliseum.

That date would turn out to be a historic one for me, but I didn't know it when the game started. Vachon again was in the net and I took a seat at the end of the bench.

I wasn't as nervous as I had been in Los Angeles because I had been with the club three days now and was starting to feel at home. Besides, I never figured to play against Oakland.

Then it happend. A shot by George Swarbrick of the Seals hit Vachon above the eye and he had to leave the game with six minutes left in the second period. I'm not saying Vachon could have continued, but he seemed relieved to quit right there because he hadn't been playing well. The Seals were leading, 3-2, at the time.

Ruel came to me at the end of the bench and said, "Tony, get in there. And don't be nervous."

Don't be nervous? Cripes, I was shaking in my pads. Only a week ago I was playing in the minors. Now he was asking me to go out

Tony as a rookie with the Canadiens.

there and face real NHL shooters for the first time. I was plenty nervous.

I went through the warmups without staining my pants and then the game resumed. With about three minutes left in the second period, Billy Hicke took a pass from Gary Jarrett and beat me from the slot right in front of the net. It was a good shot and now Oakland was leading, 4–2.

I don't remember if Ruel or any of the players said anything to me as we rested between the second and third periods. I probably wouldn't have heard them anyway.

Hicke beat me again early in the third period. This time he was lucky. He broke in on me from right wing and I came out to cut down on the angle. His shot hit the post and caromed into the net. Damn Billy Hicke.

We finally got our attack clicking in the final six minutes when Jean Beliveau and Gilles Tremblay beat Gary Smith in the Oakland net. But that only made the score respectable. We lost, 5–4, and I had to accept part of the blame. The Seals had taken only six shots at me in twenty-six minutes, but two of them went in.

It wasn't a very happy NHL debut for Tony Esposito.

I was dejected by the time the team got back to Montreal and I started to read some of the newspapers. The writers really jumped on me. They blamed me for the Oakland loss and said I was too nervous to be a major-league goalie.

One guy who helped calm me down was Ted Harris, the big defenseman whom the Canadiens eventually traded to the Minnesota North Stars.

"Don't keep worrying about that Oakland game," Ted told me. "Just hang tough. You'll get another chance."

CHAPTER XIII

GOODBYE CANADIENS

The Montreal Canadiens were perennial champions when Tony Esposito broke in with them in 1968. But they didn't always act like champions.

Two nights after making my first NHL start against the Bruins, I played against the Black Hawks in the Montreal Forum. Luck was with me that night. I beat the Hawks, 6–3, for my first victory with the Canadiens. But I was damn lucky I wasn't killed by one of Bobby Hull's shots.

Early in the first period, John Ferguson hooked Hull. They went at it pretty good and Bobby came out of it with a nasty cut. Fergy got two major penalties and a ten-minute misconduct. Bobby was back on ice after serving a five-minute major. He was mad as hell.

Late in the first period, Bobby moved in on me from left wing and let go a screen shot. I didn't see the puck until the last second. If I had moved my face a fraction of an inch, it would have gone in the net. So I just closed my eyes and prayed.

The puck hit my mask in the right cheek area and knocked me down. It was only a half-speed shot — Bobby didn't get good wood on it — and thank God for that. I was a little shook up but, thanks to the mask, I wasn't even bruised.

Now when people ask me about the importance of wearing a mask I relate that incident and tell them that if Bobby's shot had been a little harder and I wasn't wearing the mask, well, it could have killed me.

I was lucky for another reason that night. The Canadiens were really flying. They scored three goals in the second period to stake me to a 4–1 lead. Ferguson got one of them after serving his twenty minutes in the penalty box. Then Bobby Rousseau got his second goal of the game in the third period and I was home free. What a thrill that was — winning my first game in my second NHL start. Claude Ruel was happy, too. He shook my hand in the dressing room until I thought it would fall off.

Ruel started me in the next nine Montreal games; actually he had no choice. Rogie Vachon's broken hand wasn't healing as fast as the club had hoped and Ruel obviously was afraid to use Ernie Wakely.

I got my first NHL shutout against Philadelphia on December 14, and a week later I faced Phil and the Bruins for the second time — at the Montreal Forum. This game was a classic, a scoreless tie. Danny Gallivan, the Montreal broadcaster, called it "the best all-round contest played at the Forum in ten years."

What a night my wife, Marilyn, picked to witness her first NHL game. She had traveled from Houston with Mark so the three of us could be together for the Christmas holiday. We stayed at the Martinique Motor Hotel on the corner of Guy and Dorchester in Montreal.

The night before the game, Phil dropped by the hotel to visit with us. We talked about our families and about my previous games with the Canadiens. I was now unbeaten in six starts with three victories and three ties.

"Tony," he said, "I know you're still feeling your way around in this league, but I don't want you to worry. You're going great."

"Yeah, sure," I said, "I'm playing against you tomorrow night."

"I know it," Phil said. "Just play your normal game and don't get too shook. You'll make it. I know you will."

That little pep talk must have helped me because the next night I turned in as good a game as I've ever played. The Bruins took forty-one shots at me without scoring. I stopped Phil at least five times from close range. This time I had gotten the upper hand.

It was still a nerve-wracking experience. Playing against your brother is tough, especially when you're the goalie. If you're a forward like Phil you know you're going to get some chances to score. But if you're the goalie and you've got your brother shooting at you and he's one of the best in hockey, it worries you. Hell, it scares me half to death.

Look at it this way: Phil is going to get four or five good chances in every game to beat you. Multiply that by six — the six times we face each other during the regular season — and he's going to get at least thirty good cracks at me. Sooner or later he's going to beat me and make me look bad. Some people wonder if I ever ease up on my brother. That's ridiculous. I probably try harder against Phil than anybody. And I know he always gives it his best shot against me. I'd like to see him lead the league in scoring every year, but not at my expense. No, sir. If I can stop him I will.

A goalie's mental attitude and his ability to withstand pressure is always important. I worry before every game, perhaps too much at times. You work yourself into a nervous state and when that happens you can't play as well because you're too shaky.

I'm also a nervous wreck after most games. I've had a lot of trouble with my stomach. The worst part about it is that it seems to bother me more each season and this scares me.

The Bruins, of course, are capable of giving most goalies a severe case of ulcers. Even in that 1968-69 season they were awfully tough. The night after the scoreless tie at Montreal we were back playing the Bruins in Boston. They beat me, 7-5.

What a lesson I learned that night. I was sitting on a 3–0 lead late in the first period and chuckling behind my mask when Phil surprised me by tipping in a long shot by Ted Green. "Oh, well," I told myself, "Phil is getting even for last night."

Then the Bruins really socked it to me. Phil got another goal in the second period, Derek Sanderson beat me twice and set up a goal by Wayne Cashman. But the back-breaker was a goal by Bobby Orr. He rushed the length of the ice, circled behind the net and pushed a back-hander between my pads for the go-ahead goal.

Trying to evaluate that loss, my first in the NHL, I came to two conclusions. First, I eased up a little when I had that three-goal lead, a big mistake when you're playing the Bruins. You get cocky with them and they'll put goals behind you. And, secondly, I simply ran out of gas. The Bruins wore me down by taking fifty shots that night.

Phil chatted with me after the game and tried to cheer me up.

"Don't be discouraged," he said. "When we get rolling in our own rink the way we did tonight, it's tough trying to slow us down. You did your best."

"I'm not even sure about that, Phil," I said. "See you later."

When I climbed aboard the charter bus outside Boston Garden I was told thieves had broken into the bus during the game and run off with a lot of our equipment and personal effects. It had been a bad night all around.

Ruel gave us quite a sermon when we got back to Montreal. And before our next game against Toronto, somebody wrote WIN in large letters on the locker room blackboard. I had a much easier night against the Maple Leafs, handling thirty-four shots, and we won, 4–2.

This was followed by a home-and-home weekend series against New York. I beat the Rangers, 5–3, in the Forum, but they bounced back the next night, firing fifty shots at me and winning, 3–1.

By this time, two or three of the Montreal writers were really on my back. So were the fans. They read the papers and you know, if the reporters are riding a guy, the fans get on the player eventually.

One of my biggest critics then was Rocket Richard. He had this column in a French-language newspaper in Montreal, and he was jumping all over me. He kept writing I wasn't good enough to play in the NHL. Here I was a rookie, doing my best, and the Rocket should have realized this. But instead of supporting me, he was trying to put me down.

Richard was a great hockey player for the Canadiens — the best. But now he seems so bitter. He'll write things like "hockey isn't the way it used to be in my day . . . and all the current players are lousy . . ." I've never agreed with him. The game is progressing all the time. It's getting better all the time whether Richard is willing to accept it or not.

The stuff he wrote about me really bothered me. It would have annoyed any rookie trying to break in with the Canadiens.

Ruel must have been reading some of that guff, too, because he started bugging me. What the hell did he want from me? Up to the time Vachon returned to the club in early January I had started eleven games. I had won five, lost two and tied four.

But Ruel still bugged me about a few bad goals I had let in. He seemed to know his hockey but he didn't know how to handle men. He simply couldn't communicate. Maybe it was a lack of education. I think he probably realized this when he stepped down as the Canadiens' coach during the 1970-71 season.

Claude tried hard and he was good to me most of the time. He did give me my first shot in the NHL. But he never learned how to approach his players or deal with them.

I started only one other game after Vachon returned. It was against Detroit and the Red Wings wiped me out, 4–0. I mean really wiped me out. Worsley had also rejoined the club, so the Canadiens had no use for Tony Esposito. Still, they kept me in Montreal for two or three more weeks, and this made me bitter.

While Ruel and Sam Pollock were sitting on their hands, trying to decide what to do with me, I did nothing except practice with the club. Then, at game time, I'd have to get out of my uniform and watch from the stands.

Marilyn was back in Houston with Mark and about every second day I'd get a call from her. "What are they doing up there with you?" she would ask.

"I'll be damned if I know, Marilyn. Nobody seems to want to make a decision."

The Canadiens should have sent me back to Houston as soon as Worsley was well enough to play. But they had no regard for me as an individual. I was a married man with a wife and child back in Texas and I was concerned about them. The Canadiens didn't seem to care and that really irritated me.

Pollock finally shipped me back to Houston on January 27. It was good to be reunited with my family. However, I wasn't too sharp in the net and I lost three straight games for the Apollos after my return.

I had to adjust to the climate again — it was warm in Houston — and get back in shape. We couldn't use the Sam Houston Coliseum for practice because of other bookings there, so we practiced on a rink about half the size of a normal one. It was dark and dingy and it had portable sideboards. We couldn't even scrimmage there because it was so small.

Phil Myre and I alternated in goal for the rest of the regular season. I lost only one of my final eight games. In one game against Tulsa I made fifty-eight saves in a 3–2 victory.

The Apollos finished third and faced Dallas in the opening round of the Central League playoffs. When Myre was picked to start the first game I knew I was on the way out so far as the Montreal organization was concerned.

I had a better goal-allowed average than Myre. Mine was 2.42 and Myre's was 2.83. I thought I should have started the playoffs, but Sam Pollock thought differently. He was running the show from Montreal and he told our coach, Al MacNeil, to start Myre. Sam was the boss. And I was gone.

We were eliminated by Dallas in the first round. I started one game and lost it, giving up three goals. That turned out to be the last game I played for the Montreal organization.

The Canadiens then called up Myre as their third goalie for the Stanley Cup playoffs But it turned out that Myre wasn't eligible. Now the Canadiens really pulled a slick one. Floyd Curry phoned me from the Montreal office and said the Canadiens were bringing me up for the playoffs.

"But don't come to Montreal, Tony," Curry said. "We want you to go to Cleveland and practice there with the Barons. You won't be able to play in the American League playoffs, just practice."

I thought that was pretty stupid. I was with the Barons for a week, traveling with them to Quebec City, but I couldn't play. Then I realized what the Canadiens were doing. They were hiding me in case something happened to Vachon or Worsley.

And, sure enough, something did happen. Worsley hurt a hand. The Canadiens called me up from Cleveland and, suddenly, they're real nice to me. They offered me extra money, good money, to take over as their backup goalie. I'm one of the boys again.

Ruel knows I'm out of shape so he works me hard in practice. But I didn't get into a single game. Vachon was just great. He appeared in nine playoff games and had a 1.42 average. Real super.

After eliminating the Rangers in four straight, the Canadiens ran into the Bruins. This turned out to be a real tough series. It went six games and Montreal won three of them in overtime, including the decisive one.

It felt a little strange sitting on the end of the Montreal bench and watching Phil trying to beat the Canadiens. I was sort of indifferent, I suppose. I couldn't cheer for Phil, naturally, and I was thinking of that playoff money. I needed the money more than he did anyway.

Phil had a great playoff, leading all scorers with eight goals and eighteen points. But Vachon was just too tough for him and the rest of the Bruins.

The final series against St. Louis was anticlimactic. We won the first two games at home and then went out to St. Louis to have a good time. The celebration actually started before the fourth and final game. It was a piece of cake.

We had a lot of beer and champagne on the plane ride back. When we arrived at the airport in Montreal, there were about five thousand people waiting for us. It was a wild scene, so a couple of us sneaked out a side door. I hadn't contributed anything to the Canadiens' Cup victory anyway and that mob scared me.

I skipped the parade and the reception the city staged for the Canadiens for the same reason but I did attend a couple of parties with other Montreal players. I liked most of the Canadiens. Henri Richard has always been a gentleman. John Ferguson? Another nice guy. He appears tough and he is tough, but he'll help you anyway he can.

Yvan Cournoyer has always been friendly. He jokes around a lot and doesn't take himself too seriously. I think the Montreal club could use more of his type.

Jean Beliveau was an enigma to me. He's really gentle, yet he never got too close to anybody on the club. He was sort of a loner. He would say hello to you and that was it. I can't remember ever having a real conversation with the man.

Jacques Laperriere struck me the same way. Sort of moody. In the dressing room, he would never say a word. On some nights you could tell when he was going to have a bad game. He would be brooding in a corner. On other nights he would be full of fun and would play a helluva game.

I always liked Serge Savard as a hockey player. As a person, well, it's a good thing he can play hockey because I'm not sure he could make a living at anything else. Certainly not as a diplomat. He's a little too outspoken.

Savard got on national television during the 1970 Stanley Cup playoffs and really cut me up. I had a couple of bad games, which I admit, but he told the television audience I was lousy and wasn't worth a damn. How could he put the rap on me for a couple of bad games? No educated man would do that. You hear a lot about certain cliques on the Montreal team and part of this is true. The French-Canadian players converse a lot in French and I suppose this is natural because it's their native tongue. But it is upsetting to some of the other players. I think the situation worsened under Claude Ruel, which is probably why he no longer is the Montreal coach. His French was perfect but his English was poor. So, naturally, he conversed a lot in the language he knew best. And I'd have to say he was a little pro-French Canadian. He always leaned toward those players with French backgrounds and this caused a lot of trouble.

My troubles in Montreal, though, were mainly with Sam Pollock. Sam is a good hockey man — one of the best in the business. He's talented and knows how to recognize talent. He didn't recognize me, though, and that's how I wound up with the Chicago Black Hawks.

CHAPTER XIV

OUIJA MAGIC

Few athletes admit they're superstitious. Phil Esposito is. On occasion he has even consulted the ouija board. Does it help?

The four goals I scored against Tony during his trial with the Canadiens helped to remind me of a night we had spent in front of a ouija board the previous summer. The board indicated Tony would be called up by Montreal during the 1968-69 season and I would score forty-five goals for the Bruins. It had been right once. Could it be right again?

I started wondering about that when I reached the mid-season All-Star Game break with twenty-nine goals and was leading the league in scoring with sixty-seven points. Then I went to Montreal for the All-Star Game on January 21. I had been named to the East team for the first time, which was quite a thrill in itself.

When we were introduced to the crowd at the Montreal Forum and skated out on the ice, I looked down the line of players and got a small lump in my throat. My teammates were Jean Beliveau and Norm Ullman, Bobby and Dennis Hull (those buggers), Rod Gilbert, Frank Mahovlich and, of course, old Gordie Howe.

I made one discovery that night, though, that kind of surprised me. Although this was the first game since expansion that matched the East against the West All-Stars, very few guys on our team seemed to take it too seriously.

When Claude Larose, who was then with Minnesota, scored with less than three minutes left to play to give the West a 3–3 tie, I felt insulted. We should have beat those expansion guys easily. But most of the East players couldn't have cared less.

111

On his way to All-Star selection, Phil scores against Toronto.

Following the All-Star Game, we met the Red Wings at Detroit. I was blanked and the game ended in a 2–2 tie. Then I went on a crazy scoring rampage. I got twenty-five points on seven goals and eighteen assists in the next ten games. Holy cow! I now had thirty-six goals and ninety-two points in fifty-four games.

I felt certain I would get the forty-five goals the ouija board had predicted and become the league's first one hundred-point scorer. After all, I had twenty-two games left to play.

Even Punch Imlach was on my side now. He told a Toronto friend of mine after I passed the ninety-point mark that "Phil can't miss" hitting one hundred. "He has a 'nose' for the puck and is hard to move off it," Punch said. "And that reach of his. Hell, he can reach around the block with his stick."

Now wasn't that nice of Punch, that bloody front-runner?

During that ten-game streak, though, I committed an act of violence that was inexcusable. It happened in a game against the Philadelphia Flyers at Boston Garden, February 8. I swatted referee Bob Sloan.

Much has been written about that incident, most of it erroneous. Here are the facts: Sloan was having a bad night in that game. The Philly players were grabbing, clutching and holding on to me in front of the net and Sloan was letting them get away with it.

In the third period, Larry Hale and I went into the boards and came out slashing each other. Sloan gave us each two minutes and that should of been the end of it. But Hale said something to me that sounded like "You big Wop," or "You big slob," as we were skating off.

We were then near the referee's circle where Sloan was standing and I said to Hale, "Why you dirty bastard." Sloan turned around and said, "Phil, you just bought yourself a ten-minute misconduct penalty."

That's when I blew my stack. I turned on Sloan and gave him a couple of little taps. I didn't hit him that hard, but I was angry as hell. I had cursed Hale and Sloan thought I was cursing him.

Right there I was in trouble. Sloan would file his report to NHL president Clarence Campbell and only the Lord and Campbell knew what sort of a suspension he would hand me.

We won that game against the Flyers, 6–5, on a goal by Wayne

Cashman. The following night, a Sunday, I got two assists in a 2–2 tie against the Seals. Two nights later I had a five-point game — two goals and three assists — in a 7–3 victory over the Black Hawks at Boston Garden.

Mr. Campbell was waiting for me when I showed up in Montreal with the Bruins for a Saturday night game against the Canadiens — a whole week after the Hale incident. I went to the hearing in Campbell's office with our coach, Harry Sinden; then-president Weston Adams, Sr., and general manager Milt Schmidt. Sloan was there, too, along with the linesmen, Bob Frampton and Ed Butler, who had worked the game against Philly.

I figured they had stacked the deck against me when one of the linesmen claimed he heard me swear at Sloan. But the films proved the linesman was down at the other end of the ice retrieving the puck. How could he hear anything?

Then Mr. Campbell asked me about striking Sloan and I admitted I had. "But it was only a couple of little blows," I said. Mr. Campbell nodded his head and seemed to agree. He then dismissed me and said he would render a decision the following Monday.

I played against the Canadiens that night and went scoreless in a 3–1 loss. We played a television game against the Black Hawks on Sunday afternoon at Chicago and lost, 5–1. I was shut out again.

On Monday, Mr. Campbell announced I had been suspended for two games. Many people figured he had been very lenient with me, but I feel he weighed the evidence and made a fair decision. Wasn't it strange, though, that he let me play in that TV game before he arrived at his decision?

The suspension gave me a chance to take Linda and our two daughters on a vacation trip to Bermuda. I celebrated my twenty-seventh birthday while I was there, then flew out to Los Angeles to rejoin the Bruins. I had missed their 3–0 loss at Pittsburgh and a 9–0 skunking at New York.

Four straight defeats — the two before I left and the two while I was away — normally would affect any club. But the Bruins were loosey-goosey when I showed up in Los Angeles. I came in for a lot of friendly joshing.

"Here comes one-punch Phil," Freddy Stanfield said.

"Yeah," said Teddy Green, "the big man has returned."

It was good to be back. It felt so good I went out and set up a pair of third-period goals by John McKenzie that gave us a 4–2 victory over the Kings. The following night I got a goal and two assists in a 9–0 victory over the Seals at Oakland.

In two games I had picked up five points to equal the single-season record of ninety-seven shared by my two old Chicago buddies, Bobby Hull and Stan Mikita. Screw Bob Sloan. And screw Larry Hale. We were flying back to Boston and that's where I wanted to bust that record.

I did it in a game against the Rangers at Boston Garden. It was a Saturday night, March 1, 1969. The date stands out in my mind for several reasons. First, my parents were visiting me and Linda. My mother had been having some heart trouble and dad took her to a Boston clinic for a check-up. She remained there while my father came with me to the game. It was the first time he saw me in a Boston uniform.

In five previous games against the Rangers that season I had failed to score a single goal. This was bugging me a little, plus the fact that I was worried about my mother. Dad sensed this and said, "Don't worry, Phil, your mother is going to be okay. Just go out there and play your best."

I had seven shots at Ed Giacomin in the first period and that gray-haired sonofagun stopped 'em all. After three more unsuccessful cracks at him in the second period, I came out on the ice with Ken Hodge to kill a penalty to Ted Green. There were about seven minutes left in the period when Ken flicked the puck away from Jim Neilson in the New York end and passed it to me.

Giacomin started to move out of the net and I was between him and Bob Nevin when I got my stick on the puck, turned and shot. Eddie went down and the puck went between his pads and into the net.

That was it — my ninety-eighth point of the season. And I had gotten it by finally beating an old nemesis, Ed Giacomin. The voice of Frank Fallon, the Garden announcer, came over the public address system: "Boston goal . . . and an NHL point-scoring record . . . Phil Esposito." Everybody went wild. It was like a scene out of an old movie about Roman gladiators.

Hats were thrown on the ice and the crowd was yelling, "We

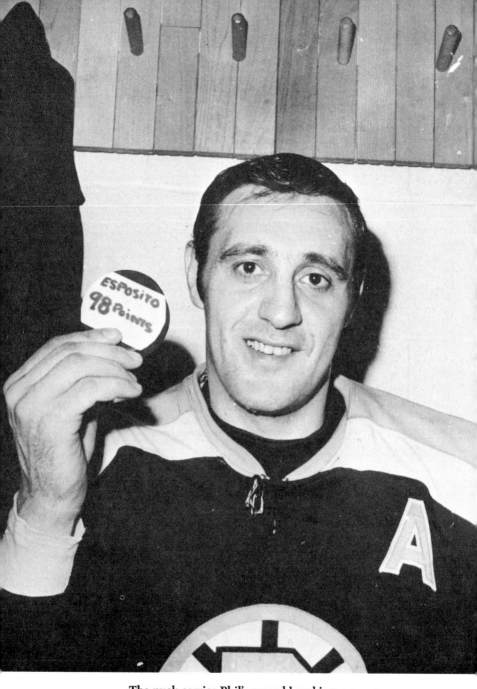

The puck carries Phil's record-breaking message.

want Espo, we want Espo." I was back on the Boston bench, getting my hair mussed and my back slapped by every Bruin player. I was physically and mentally exhausted. My arms were aching and my feet hurt. The Rangers, trailing by 6–2 at that point, took out Giacomin and replaced him with Don Simmons. While Simmons was going through his warmup, I skated back on the ice and the crowd was yelling and I had a wonderful feeling. I had heard the fans yell like that for Bobby Hull when he scored his fifty-fourth goal to break Rocket Richard's record and now I was getting the same treatment.

As I skated past the New York bench, I thanked Giacomin for handing me the puck after my goal. He said, "You're welcome, Phil, and if you wind up with an extra picture of that goal I'd like to have it, eh." I'm ashamed to admit this, but I never got a copy of that picture for Eddie. One day I will, I promise.

With Simmons now in the New York net and time running out in the second period, I set up a goal by Bobby Orr. That gave me ninety-nine points on thirty-eight goals and sixty-one assists. I had a whole period left to make it one hundred, but I was too pooped to pop. The game ended with us winning, 8–5, and my dad and I hurried home to check on my mother's condition. She was fine.

The following night we played the Pittsburgh Penguins at the Garden. My dad remained behind with my mother, listening to the game on the radio. Joe Daley was the Pittsburgh goaltender and he did a good job over the first two periods. I had two shots and no goals.

As we came on the ice for the third period, a young boy yelled, "Please get that one hundredth point, Phil. I want to be able to say I saw it." He saw it with seventeen seconds gone in the final period. Green flipped the puck up ice to Hodge and Ken relayed it to me as I cut in from the left side. Daley moved to his right, hit the ice and I slipped it underneath him.

That was another historic moment for me. I had become the first one hundred-point man in NHL history. The reception I got from the fans was just as wild as the one the previous night. They tossed everything on the ice — hats and caps, rolled-up programs and a white football helmet.

Then, just as the Garden's clean-up crew was completing its work, a pink brassiere was flung from the east side of the arena and landed on the ice. Now there was a real fan.

I beat Daley again six minutes later while Hodge and I were killing a penalty to Rick Smith. Kenny set it up again with a super pass. I broke in from the right this time, pulled Daley and popped it behind him. That gave me forty goals and one hundred and one points and helped wrap up a 4–0 win over the Penguins.

In our next game against Detroit, I set up both of our goals in a 2–2 tie to crack another record. I now had sixty-three assists, one more than Stan Mikita got when we were teammates in Chicago two years earlier. I went on to finish the regular season with forty-nine goals and seventy-seven assists for one hundred twenty-six points.

The ouija board had been right again. It also had predicted we would finish second and that's exactly where we wound up, three points back of Montreal.

Our opponent in the opening round of the playoffs was Toronto. I remember people predicting we couldn't beat the Maple Leafs because they were more experienced and always were tough in the playoffs. And, besides, didn't Phil Esposito always choke at playoff time?

Well, I didn't choke in the opening game. I scored the first time I got on the ice and set up a goal by John Bucyk two minutes later. I tied a playoff record that night with four goals and two assists as we creamed the Leafs, 10–0. I had finally snapped my playoff jinx and I felt great about that.

Hodge and Ron Murphy did all the work, clearing paths for me like linemen on a football team. I remember one goal where I had the puck in a corner to the right of Toronto goalie Bruce Gamble. Murphy was in front of the net with one defenseman and Hodge was in front with the other. I think the defensemen were Tim Horton and Jim Dorey.

Horton was holding Murph and Murph grabbed him. Hodge and Dorey were grabbing each other. Nobody was near me. I stick-handled out of the corner and had all sorts of time and room to shoot. So I took my time, pulled Gamble out and put it in the net.

I think I could have taken another thirty seconds to fool around with the puck. That was really something.

People still talk about that game for another reason. It was one of the wildest in Stanley Cup history. There were one hundred thirty-two minutes in penalties, seventy-six against Toronto and fifty-six against the Bruins.

The madness started in the second period when Pat Quinn gave Orr a vicious elbow check. Bobby had picked the puck up behind the net and was skating up along the right side when Quinn caught him with his head down. I thought it was a dirty check. Quinn is a big man and he sort of jumped up and gave Bobby quite an elbow.

Bobby went down and was really dazed. The Boston fans are as rabid as they come, you know, and they were yelling like crazy when Quinn went to the penalty box. Some fans smashed the glass partition separating the penalty box from the mezzanine seats. This scared hell out of me and I rushed over to Davey Keon, the Toronto captain.

"You better get Quinn out of there, Davey, before those people try to kill him," I said.

I was sure they would try, too. They had already tried.

Keon said, "Okay, Phil, I'll do what I can."

He went to the penalty box, talked to Quinn and eventually got Pat to go to the dressing room.

But that was only the beginning. All hell broke loose in the third period. It started between our goalie, Gerry Cheevers, and Forbes Kennedy. Cheesy has this habit of whacking at guys he dislikes with his stick. He didn't like Kennedy.

With about four minutes left to play, Kennedy skated in front of the net and Cheesy took a whack at him. Then Kennedy jumped Cheesy, who isn't known for his fighting capabilities. He's a good goaltender but not much of a fighter, something like me. They exchanged a couple of swings and then our other goalie, Ed Johnston, rushed off the bench to help. They were joined by Gamble and Johnny Bower. What a scene that was. All four goal-tenders in the middle of the brawl.

Ted Green took a couple of shots at Kennedy, who looked as

if he was going nuts. But it was Johnny McKenzie who did the best job on Kennedy. Pie, who is quite a needler, got Kennedy at center ice and gave him a good working over.

They finally got Kennedy off the ice, but not before he slugged linesman George Ashley. Kennedy was suspended for four games and fined a thousand dollars. He never played another game in the NHL.

Looking back on that fracas now I can't help but think Punch Imlach was behind it. I don't like saying that, but those are my true feelings. There were circumstances which I can't fully explain, but playing hockey you can tell at times when a guy is acting on orders. Imlach really had his club aroused. Not the good players, you understand, but by the time the Leafs were down, 6–0, I feel he put Kennedy out there to try and maim one of us.

That's bad business. I don't like to see a coach do that. However, that's the way Punch is.

I have one other scary memory of that game. A real tough guy came up to me after the game and asked if I would like Quinn "wiped out." I was shocked. In underground terms he was offering me a murder "contract."

"Man," I told him, "I don't know you and I don't want to know you. Don't talk to me, leave me alone and get the hell out of here."

I've never seen the guy again. Even if I did I'm not sure I would recognize him. But there's no doubt in my mind he was a real torpedo.

We whipped the Leafs again, 7–0, in the second game, then went to Toronto, where we have always had trouble winning. We were still flying high and wiped them out in four games.

I had become sick and tired of people saying I wasn't a clutch player, so you can imagine how happy I was when I got six goals and four assists in the four games against Toronto. I had finally shown Tommy Ivan and Billy Reay I was a playoff performer.

Following that series, the Maple Leafs fired Imlach. I didn't wire him my condolences.

The Canadiens had wiped out the Rangers in their opening series, so they were just as hot when we showed up in Montreal. Tony had been recalled by the Canadiens as their backup goalie. We met and chatted only once. The Bruins were staying at the

Martinique and Tony was there with Mickey Redmond and Ernie Hicke.

One night we sat in his hotel room, had a few beers and joked around. We talked very little hockey. Tony didn't figure to play against us anyway, and he didn't.

We dropped the first two games in Montreal, then won the next two at Boston. I had my best night in the third game when I scored twice and set up three more goals in a 5–0 victory. I didn't score another goal and we were eliminated in six games. The sixth game at Boston was a heart-breaker. Jean Beliveau won it with a goal in the second overtime period.

Ralph Backstrom did quite a job in shadowing me through most of the series. I must admit he has always checked me pretty well. The reason he does is that Ralph doesn't worry about scoring. He just makes sure that I don't score. He's also a shifty kind of guy and gets away with stuff that the referees either ignore or don't detect, like grabbing my stick and all that jazz.

Despite Backstrom's close-checking, I wound up as the leading scorer in the playoffs with eight goals and ten assists for eighteen points. That was three more than Beliveau accumulated in leading the Canadiens to the championship.

So it had been a great season. I had won the Ross Trophy as the league's leading scorer and the Hart Trophy as the league's Most Valuable Player.

When I went back home to the Soo that summer, a man approached me on the street and congratulated me for scoring one hundred twenty-six points. My father, who was with me, turned to the man and said, "Philly can do better . . . just you watch."

He was right, too.

CHAPTER XV

UNDER THE TABLE

Two years after the Chicago Black Hawks ped-
dled Phil Esposito to Boston, Tommy Ivan reached
into hockey's grab bag — the player draft — and
pulled out Tony Esposito. The Chicago general man-
ager, who had been castigated for allowing Phil to
escape to Boston, was complimented for drafting the
younger Esposito. Ivan, though, received help from
unexpected quarters before the 1969 draft meetings,
according to Tony.

I have always entertained the thought I wound up with the
Black Hawks through a pre-arranged deal. It involved the Hawks,
the Montreal Canadiens and the Minnesota North Stars. Here's
how I feel it happened:

Sam Pollock of the Canadiens wasn't sure I was a major-league
goalie. It mattered little to him that I had given up only thirty-two
goals in twelve starts and had two shutouts in my two-month trial
with the club during the 1968-69 season. Sam simply had doubts
about my talents.

Sometime between the end of the Stanley Cup playoffs in May
and the draft meetings in June, Pollock had to reach a decision
on the two goalies he would carry on Montreal's list. I figured he
would leave Gump Worsley unprotected for a couple of reasons.
First, there was Gump's age. He was then forty. And, secondly,
there was friction between Gump and Claude Ruel. They never
hit it off too well, primarily because Gump never worked too hard
in practice and was always complaining.

Pollock, though, had other ideas. He went to the 1969 draft

meetings in Montreal prepared to protect Rogatien Vachon and Worsley. He was willing to sacrifice me for the thirty thousand dollar draft price.

This is where Chicago and Minnesota entered the picture. Wren Blair, the general manager of the North Stars, was guaranteed the first pick in the draft because his team had finished with the worst record in the NHL during the 1968-69 season. Tommy Ivan of the Black Hawks would pick second.

Blair learned just befort the draft meeting that Pollock had made a deal with Ivan which would permit the Black Hawks to draft me. But Pollock first required Blair's cooperation. Sam worked that out neatly. He got Blair to by-pass me in the draft as final payment for Danny O'Shea, whom the North Stars had acquired from the Canadiens in an earlier deal.

Blair, his hands now tied by Pollock, made Dick Sentes, a mediocre Montreal farmhand, his first pick. Ivan completed this under-the-table maneuver by drafting me. Sentes, by the way, failed to make the North Stars and wound up back in the minors.

When Phil heard the Black Hawks had drafted me he offered his condolences.

"If you think you had trouble discussing money with Pollock, wait until you sit down with Ivan," he said. "Tommy is a real tough bargainer."

Phil was only half kidding. He was happy I was joining his old team and so was I. With the Black Hawks I knew I would get greater opportunities to play and prove to them and myself that I was a major-league goalie.

The move to Chicago also provided me with the chance to make more money, especially when it came to endorsements. In Montreal I didn't have that opportunity because I don't speak French well and the outside money usually went to the French-Canadian stars like Jean Beliveau and Henri Richard. They were the big heroes among the French-speaking people in Montreal.

But I have always been obliged to the Montreal club for giving me my first chance to play in the NHL. It has taken some goalies many years to make it. The Canadiens gave me a crack at it in my second year as a pro and I appreciated that.

Ivan was as tough as Phil predicted when we discussed my

contract at the Hawks' training camp at St. Catherines. But I respected him and with a little help from Alan Eagleson, the attorney for the NHL Players Association, I finally accepted Ivan's terms.

It was a reasonably good contract — especially since I was still regarded as a rookie in the NHL. My base salary was twenty thousand. I also had bonus clauses guaranteeing me one hundred dollars for each shutout, one thousand if the Hawks finished first or second, another thousand if my goals-allowed average was 3.00 or better, and twenty-five hundred dollars if I appeared in thirty-five games.

Denis DeJordy was the Hawks' number one goalie when I showed up in camp. He had put in a rough year with the Hawks the previous season. The Chicago fans were disgusted with the club for finishing last and they rode Denis something awful. It must have been a nerve-wracking experience.

Denis and I shared the goaltending in most of the exhibition games. He'd work a period or two and I'd finish up or vice-versa. I had a great training camp, giving up only thirteen goals in eleven games. Ivan was impressed and so was coach Billy Reay.

The night before our season-opening game at St. Louis, Reay decided to start me instead of DeJordy. Billy had real confidence in me and told me so.

"I'm starting you, Tony, because of the way you played in the exhibition games," he said. "Now try not to worry too much. I feel you can get the job done, so don't disappoint me."

I couldn't help wondering then how Phil had had so much trouble satisfying Reay when he was with the Black Hawks. To me, Billy is an expert coach. He's also an expert psychologist. He knows how to treat his players. If a guy needs a pat on the back, Billy will give him that pat and say things like "That's the way to play," or "Great game, pal, keep it up." And if a player needs to get bawled out, Billy will do that, too, and tell him, "You'd better shape up or else."

Going into my first game with the Black Hawks at St. Louis I was pretty nervous. I had put in that stint with Montreal, but I felt I still had to prove I belonged in the league.

The only thing I proved that night was that Billy Reay may

Tony got a new uniform, but Phil was still on the other side.

have been unwise in starting me. The Blues bombed me, 7–2, scoring three goals in less than three minutes in the final period. What a debut!

Gerry Pinder, who was also playing in his first game with the Black Hawks, scored two goals. His second came early in the final period and cut the Blues' lead to 3–2. Even when Frank St. Marseille beat me at 8:45 I figured we'd bounce back.

Then the roof of the St. Louis Arena fell in on me — or so it seemed. Phil Goyette, that shifty old rascal, fooled me from close range at 10:34; Jim Roberts scored at 12:16 and Jean Guy Talbot popped one in at 13:30. After each goal, the Blues' fans whooped it up with a chorus of "When the Saints Go Marching In."

I was singing my own version of the blues after the game. My pride was hurt, especially when Reay told me he thought I quit on him in the third period. This made me a little angry, but maybe I didn't try as hard as I should have. Reay calmed down later and came to me and said, "Forget it, Tony. Just keep working and it will come."

Denis DeJordy told me the same thing. "It's only one game," he said. "You'll show 'em the next time."

DeJordy was in the nets for our home opener the following night and we lost to Oakland, 2–1. Denis played well and I figured he would start the next game against the Detroit Red Wings. But Reay threw me right back in the cage. I collapsed again in the third period, gave up three goals, and we lost, 4–1.

The goal that really broke my heart was a shot by Gordie Howe. He took a pass from Alex Delvecchio and cut across the blue line, then fired. It was a typical Howe wrist shot. As I moved to stop it, the puck hit a bump in the ice and bounced past me. Damn, I was mad. We blew the game right there. I blew it anyway. The team played well enough. It was just me.

In the final minutes, the Chicago Stadium crowd started chanting, "We want Bobby, we want Bobby." We wanted Bobby Hull, too, but he was then squabbling with management over his contract and was back home in Ontario.

Then, as the game ended, the fans serenaded Reay with "So long, Billy, we hate to see you go." They were picking on the wrong man. Our coach didn't lose that game to Detroit. I did.

Reay didn't criticize me this time. Instead, he reminded some of the reporters he had a young team on his hands and rookies were bound to make mistakes. We had seven rookies then. In addition to me and Pinder, there were Cliff Koroll, Jim Wiste and Keith Magnuson, all graduates of the University of Denver, Terry Caffery and Paul Shmyr.

"We've got a bunch of youngsters who are not used to working with each other," Reay said. "And kids get flustered, especially on home ice with the crowd yelling at them."

I was one of his most flustered newcomers. And I was really worried. I had lost my first two starts and now my confidence was shattered. I didn't know if I could play in the league.

Phil phoned me that week and tried to cheer me up. He could tell by the sound of my voice that I was downhearted.

"Don't worry so damn much, Bomby," he said. "Just hang in there and get yourself ready for the next game."

Reay used DeJordy in the next three games. We lost to Toronto and Minnesota and tied New York. Six games and no victories. Then we went to Montreal for a Saturday night game and Reay gave me the assignment.

I was a bundle of nerves when we showed up at the Montreal Forum. I had given up eleven goals in my first two starts and now I was going against my old Montreal teammates. They knew me and I knew them. Who would have the advantage?

Then somebody reminded me that the Canadiens were unbeaten in twenty-four straight games at home. God, was I worried. I got into the net at the start of the game and I wondered to myself, "How long can I hold them?" and "Will they embarrass the hell out of me?" I also remembered Phil's advice to "hang in there."

And that's just what I did. I was hanging in there, playing one period at a time, and before I knew it we were in the third period and were ahead, 5–0. Now I'm sweating harder than ever because I wanted that shutout.

The Canadiens were so frustrated by that time that they abandoned their usual style of crisp, lead passes and were dumping the puck in our zone and sending their forwards in to chase it. But our defensemen — Magnuson, Doug Jarrett, Gilles Marotte and Pat Stapleton — were beating them to the puck and clearing it to center ice.

Claude Ruel, my old coach, was blowing his cool. He was pacing back and forth behind the Montreal bench and shouting, "Skate, skate, skate, you guys. Get the puck, there it is, get the damn puck."

But our team controlled the puck so well during that final period that the Canadiens took only five shots. I handled them all and wound up with thirty saves and a 5–0 victory. Geez, did we celebrate. The beer we had after the game tasted like beer again.

We had snapped the Canadiens' home unbeaten streak and handed them their first defeat of the season. And after seven games, we finally had our first victory. Billy Reay complimented me on the shutout and said, "Tony, I think we're ready to roll now."

I felt like the whole world had been lifted off my shoulders. The pressure on me prior to the game had been tremendous. I hadn't played well in my first two starts and then I was thrown in against a team I had been with the previous season. But I came out of it smiling again because I had shown myself and my coach I could handle pressure.

We traveled out to the West, dropped a 3–1 game at Oakland, then started to roll as Reay had predicted. I started the next six games and we won them all. I picked up two more shutouts — against Toronto and Montreal — and gave up only five goals in the other four games.

My second shutout against Montreal was a 1–0 job. It was a humdinger. Rogie Vachon had us shut out until Stan Mikita tipped in a shot by Gerry Pinder with less than three minutes left. I made stick saves on Jacques Lemaire and Mickey Redmond in the next two minutes, then Vachon was lifted for an extra forward.

Bobby Rousseau picked up a loose puck right in front of me and flicked it. The puck hit about two feet up on the left post and bounced out. Rousseau raised his stick in the air as if he had scored and the Canadiens went nuts when John Ashley, the referee, ruled it didn't go in. He was right, of course. It wasn't a hard shot so there was no way it could have bounced out like that unless it hit the post.

Rousseau gave Ashley a lot of lip and this surprised me. Bobby has always been a good hockey player but he seemed to lack aggressiveness. He never did mix it up very much. That's probably why the Canadiens eventually traded him to Minnesota. Then he wound up in New York. But on this night he was plenty aggressive. He thought the puck went in. He probably still thinks so. Following that game, Reay paid me another compliment. Talking to some reporters in his office, he said, "I can't recall any time since I've been coaching here when we've gotten such consistently fine goaltending as Tony has given us in the last six games." That made me feel good. Like any other guy doing a job, I like the boss to express confidence in me once in a while.

Our whole club now was in good spirits. We had bounced back from our miserable start and we were playing great hockey.

Then, on the night of November 19, the big man came back. Bobby Hull walked into our dressing room at Chicago Stadium before a game against the Rangers and said, "I'm ready to play, gang." Actually, he was a little out of shape and he knew it. What the hell, he had missed the entire training camp and the first fourteen games of the regular season while squabbling over his contract. Not even Bobby Hull can spot the guys two months of conditioning and expect to skate rings around them.

It was good, though, to have Bobby back. We had been winning without him, but we were really worried during his long holdout. We needed that man in the lineup. Look at it this way: If Bobby scores fifty goals in a season and sets up another fifty, he's contributing more than a point a game. You can't overlook that kind of help. I think management realized this because we couldn't go on forever without him.

Yet, I feel Bobby was foolish for holding out so long. He was obligated by his contract to play. He either had to stick by his contract or quit. I know if I faced a decision like that I would give it considerable thought and once I made my decision, I would stick to it.

Bobby's action cost him a lot of bad publicity and substantial financial loss. The club fined him fifteen hundred dollars for each game he missed. So he came back because he had to. He's got many investments, many enterprises, and he needed the cash to protect those investments.

When he walked into the locker room before that Ranger game

there was no animosity toward him. We all knew the story and why he was there. And how can you dislike Bobby Hull? He is such an easy guy to get along with. And, with that personality of his he can soft-soap anybody.

Some of the guys did kid him, however. They said things like "Where have you been, Bobby? Out selling your cattle?" Or "You got back just in time, Bob. We almost raffled off your equipment." Bobby laughed it all off. Then he skated out on the ice and got a mixed reaction — some cheers and some boos — from the Chicago fans.

We tied the Rangers that night, 1–1, with me in goal. Bobby took seven shots. Three were on target but were stopped by Ed Giacomin. Four others were blocked in front. Some of the fans booed him because they figured he would be the old Bobby, go crazy and score two or three goals. But he tired fast because he wasn't in shape. He was real beat at the end of the game.

Bobby was blanked again in our next game — a 2–2 tie with the Bruins. He finally found the range with a power play goal against the Pittsburgh Penguins that helped us to a 3–2 victory and he scored again in our 8–0 rout of Los Angeles. We were now unbeaten in ten straight games but because of our early slump we were down in fourth place.

In those ten games (eight victories, two ties) I had allowed only ten goals to lower my average to 1.64. I was as hot as a pistol. Gordie Howe, though, helped to cool me off. That old bugger figured in two goals as the Red Wings beat me, 5–4, to snap our unbeaten streak. Oh, well, you can't win 'em all.

We went to Boston for a game early in December and Reay yanked me in the third period after I had given up four goals, one to Phil. This didn't embarrass me as much as a game I played four nights later at Minnesota when the North Stars scored eight goals against me. That one was a real stinker.

I dread playing in Minnesota, mainly because we stay at a motel near the rink. It's way out in the sticks and before a game you can't find anything to do to kill the time. You can't even go to a movie. Before that eight-goal game there, I did nothing but sleep. By game time I was real groggy.

The first shot the North Stars took at me was a good one by

Billy Collins and it went in. Now I was all shook up and they poured it on. Fern Rivard must have been sleeping in the Minnesota net, too, because at the end of the second period the score was tied, 5–5. Then Bill Goldsworthy beat me twice in eleven seconds and that really teed me off.

I put in another bad night in my next game at Montreal and was yanked again after giving up four goals. I could have lost all my confidence right there and been in real trouble. But Reay kept encouraging me and playing me.

Then, early in January, I got hot again. I won six straight and had three shutouts, giving me ten for the first half of the season. I was the leader in the race for the Vezina Trophy and I was named to the Eastern Division All-Star team. That meant I would be playing on the same team with Phil in the All-Star Game at St. Louis.

Not bad for a goalie the Canadiens discarded.

CHAPTER XVI

BLOOD MONEY

The 1969-70 NHL season was marked by a dollar war, a near-tragic stick-swinging duel and a unique All-Star Game. All touched the lives of the Espositos, especially Phil.

Most professional athletes avoid discussing their salaries for various reasons. Some are overpaid and they know it. Some are underpaid and they don't want the general public to know it.

There are other little intrigues involved in the signing of a superstar. Many teams "leak" contract figures to the press which are inflated and the player, out of pride, remains silent because he doesn't want to embarrass the club and himself.

In my dealings with newspapermen I have always side-stepped any questions dealing with my salary, but not for any of the above reasons. I simply felt that what Phil Esposito was earning was Phil Esposito's business and nobody else's. I have never asked a newspaperman how much his paper was paying him.

But I feel now is a good time to straighten out a few misconceptions that have made the rounds regarding my salary negotiations with the Bruins.

First, I feel that the Boston club has always treated me well. And Charley Mulcahy, the Bruins' attorney who handles most of the contract negotiations, is one of the fairest men I've ever met. He has a job to do. I don't think he likes it. I think he'd like to give us players every cent we ask for, but he gets paid by the Bruins to get us to sign for as little as possible.

All members of the Bruins know this. Charley knows this. I have always had the feeling when discussing a contract with Charley

Mulcahy that he'd like to say, "Phil, I know you're worth every cent you're demanding, so take it." But he can't. Instead, he gives me a silly grin and a sheepish look and says, "Phil, don't be ridiculous. You're asking for the world."

Charley Mulcahy is a smart man and a man I have come to respect. In fact, I'd like to make a prediction now regarding this man: I personally feel he'll become the president of the National Hockey League when Clarence Campbell retires. He is the general counsel for the league, he is well-liked by the NHL Players Association, management and the Board of Governors.

When I joined the Bruins in 1967, they inherited my Chicago contract which guaranteed me eighteen thousand five hundred for the second year of a two-year contract. That was all they were obliged to pay me then, but the Bruins gave me a four thousand dollar raise. Following my first season in Boston, I signed a one hundred twenty thousand dollar contract for three years. At the time I figured it was a good contract. What the hell, it amounted to almost a one hundred per cent raise.

Under the terms of the contract, my take-home pay was twenty thousand a year. The remaining sixty thousand will be handled in deferred payments and I can't collect on that until 1978. Then the Bruins will pay me twenty thousand dollars a year for three years.

Reviewing that contract later I came to one startling conclusion: I wasn't able to collect interest on the deferred sixty thousand. The money is dormant. This is where the Bruins were smart. I didn't ask for interest on the money and they didn't offer it to me. The mistake I made then was not soliciting the help of a tax consultant or a smart attorney like Alan Eagleson, the head of the NHL Players Association.

But the important thing is that if I'm not playing hockey when those deferred payments come due and I'm only making about fifteen thousand a year, well, the added twenty thousand a year for three years will be a big help.

By that time I'm sure I'll be retired as a player. I don't want to play hockey like Gordie Howe until I'm eighty-five or ninety years old. I'd like to quit around thirty-four or thirty-five. Linda and I talk about this a lot, about having more children later and growing up with them. I haven't had a chance to watch my two daughters grow and this bugs me a lot.

If I do stick to those plans and retire when I'm thirty-five, my oldest daughter, Laurie, will be a teenager and I'd like to be there to watch over her. No guys are going to get fresh with her without me knowing about it.

Getting back to that three-year contract, it was unfortunate in a way that I signed it the season I became the first player to score more than one hundred points. I talked it over with Charley Mulcahy at the end of the 1968-69 season. I wanted to re-negotiate the contract, but Charley said it couldn't be done.

This is when some of the Boston papers were printing stories that I was a holdout. It was just before the opening of training camp in 1969. I was disappointed with the Bruins for not offering to rewrite the contract. I felt they were legally right but morally wrong.

Still, I never seriously considered holding out for a very good reason. The Bruins — and I have never revealed this before — gave me a good bonus at the end of the 1968-69 season. I didn't ask for it, but they gave it to me anyway.

I also earned about fifteen thousand dollars additional that year in award money. There was the Most Valuable Player award and the scoring championship, first team All-Star and the playoff money. So with the Bruins' bonus and all, I picked up more than twenty-five thousand extra. That wasn't bad pickin's.

While I'm on the subject of money, I feel I should point out here how things have changed in recent years for hockey players in the area of endorsements. There was a time — and it wasn't too long ago — when even superstars like Gordie Howe and Bobby Hull and Jean Beliveau would settle for peanuts, or a suit of clothes, for the use of their names on hockey equipment and related products.

This changed with (a) expansion and (b) the introduction of astute business managers like Fred Sharf who took over the management of the players' outside interests and helped them realize how they were being short-changed in comparison to the fees earned by other pro athletes.

I first met Fred Sharf during the 1968-69 season when I was on my way to my first record-breaking year with the Bruins. He's a Boston native, a Harvard graduate and is familiar with the merchandising of sporting goods. His family has been involved as importers, distributors and manufacturers of sports equipment since 1896. The family factory, known as M. Sharf & Co., is located in the Boston suburb of Somerville, and that's my business address, too.

Fred helped me form the Phil Esposito Management Corporation, and I have reached the point now where I have been able to double my salary with the Bruins through careful use of my name on almost any business venture you can name.

And I have ranged far beyond the endorsement of hockey equipment. My name has been used as a sort of "silent salesman" for companies dealing in lip ointment, air travel, magnetic tape, breakfast foods, spark plugs, razor blades, clothing, and the use of natural gas as a home-heating fuel.

It has all proved quite profitable for myself and for Tony, who also employs Fred Sharf as his business agent. Tony and I also run hockey schools in the Boston area and in the Soo during the off-season, so we don't get too much time to sit around and rest in the summer.

The holdout stories were big news when the Bruins opened their training camp without me in September, 1969. But I was late getting to camp because I had a strep throat. I wasn't a holdout.

That throat infection really knocked me flat on my ass. I had never been so sick. One day I couldn't even get out of bed. I was dizzy, then everything went black.

"Geez, I feel awful," I told Linda. "I can't swallow and I'm worried about that and the dizzy spells."

Linda got alarmed, too. "We better get you to a doctor," she said.

I probably never should have left the house, but I climbed into our car, driven by my friend, Sheriff Roger Wells, and went to the office of Dr. Donald Barkan. He didn't like my looks as soon as I walked in. After a quick examination, he said, "Phil, it's lucky you finally decided you needed a doctor. The infection is getting quite serious."

He told me my kidneys had been affected and ordered complete rest. I went home to bed and didn't leave it for a week. When I finally recovered, I headed for the Bruins' training camp in London, Ontario. I was far behind the other guys in conditioning and had to do some fast catching up.

By the time our third exhibition game rolled around I was ready to go. It was against the St. Louis Blues at Ottawa on September 21, 1969, a Sunday night. It was a game I wish I had missed.

The referee that night was Ken Bodendistel. He called a minor penalty against me early in the game and he claimed I pushed him. I didn't. I was following him across the ice to protest the penalty when he stopped in his tracks and I ran into him.

That little incident cost me a two hundred fifty dollar fine. But another incident that happened later in the game almost cost Teddy Green his life.

Greenie and Wayne Maki jostled each other in a corner and Greenie came out swinging. He caught Maki with a good left hook. Wayne got up and speared Greenie in the stomach. Greenie then swung his stick and missed. I figured it would end right there and it would have if Bodendistel and the linesmen had moved faster.

Maybe this is a terrible thing to say, putting a guy on the spot, but Bodendistel was standing right there and should have taken quick action. He didn't and, maybe five or six seconds later, Maki caught Greenie looking the other way, swung his stick and crunched Teddy over the head. He went down like a felled ox.

I was one of the first guys at Greenie's side. His face was twisted and he was foaming at the mouth. I tried to lift him by the left arm, but the arm was paralyzed. I turned to our trainer, Danny Canney, and said, "Get Greenie to a hospital. Get him out of here quick."

Greenie was trying to get up and kept saying, "Where is he? I'll kill the sonofabitch. I'll kill him." He kept trying to push me away but he couldn't because he was paralyzed.

After they carried Greenie off the ice and to the hospital, Wayne Maki got me real mad. He's from my home town and I grew up with him, but this wasn't the same kid I remembered back in the Soo. He was like a mad man.

Bobby Orr went up to him and said something like "We're going to get you, Maki." Wayne swung his stick again and just missed me by inches because I was standing between him and Orr.

It scared the hell out of me. Al Arbour, the St. Louis defenseman, was standing next to me.

"You'd better get Wayne out of here," I said, "before something else happens."

"Jesus, we'd better," Al said.

He grabbed Wayne and led him off the ice. Wayne was scared. You could see it in his eyes. But to swing that stick like that. Man, that was brutal.

Greenie needed three delicate brain operations to repair the damage caused by Maki's stick. The skull fracture he suffered was so severe that bone fragments shattered by the blow were driven into the brain.

Needless to say, our entire team was unnerved by the loss of Teddy. Then we were hit by other injuries. Derek Sanderson and Orr had knee problems, Ken Hodge and Ron Murphy suffered eye injuries, Freddy Stanfield bruised an ankle and Hodge went into a hospital for an appendectomy.

We were in pretty bad shape by the time we opened our 1969-70 season against the Rangers at Boston Garden. However, we managed to beat the Rangers, 2–1, behind some great goaltending by Eddie Johnston. This was important to us, getting off to a winning start against the club that figured to give us plenty of trouble during the season.

Then, as some of our wounded players returned, we started to really roll. We went unbeaten in our first seven games. Orr was off to a great start, too, averaging two points a game.

By the time we hit the All-Star Game break in January, Orr was leading the league in scoring with sixty-one points and I was second with forty-nine. My brother was doing pretty well, too. So well, in fact, that he joined me on the East All-Star team.

The 1970 NHL All-Star Game at St. Louis provided another historic moment in the life of the Espositos. For the first time since their juvenile hockey days in Sault Ste. Marie, a matter of ten years, they were teammates. Tony, the rookie, outshone his brother.

Phil and Tony were teammates, but only for one game.

Phil and I enjoyed a reunion with my dad the night before the All-Star Game. It was quite an occasion. Abbie Naccarato, our old coach, had made the trip from the Soo with my dad. We all checked into the Chase Hotel in St. Louis where the annual awards dinner was held on the eve of the game.

The dinner was a dragged-out affair. When it was over, Phil and I got together with my dad and Abbie for a little beer drinking. There was plenty of beer in my dad's room. Phil and I made sure of that.

I was dragging by the end of the evening; the long dinner, the food and the beer left me groggy. As a rookie approaching his first All-Star Game I suppose I should have been a little nervous, but I didn't toss and turn in bed that night. I was too damn tired to worry.

The morning of the game we went to the St. Louis Arena for a team meeting. Claude Ruel, my old Montreal coach, was there. He was coaching the East squad. Good old Claude. I had been a sub goalie for him the previous season and now I was an All-Star.

Phil and I posed for some pictures, then Bobby Hull joined us. That made a great picture. I have a huge enlargement of that one. Phil has one, too, and we gave one to our parents.

We went back to the Chase and killed a little time gabbing and napping, then returned to the Arena for the game. Ruel didn't bother giving us too many instructions. He didn't have to. The West team had pulled off an upset the previous year at Montreal by tying the East, 3–3. This time it would be different. We were going to sock it to those expansion guys.

Bobby Hull was great that night. He scored one goal and set up another by Gordie Howe and we won, 4–1. Phil was shut out and I kidded him a little about that. I took over for Ed Giacomin midway in the game and Jacques Plante relieved Bernie Parent in the West goal.

While I was warming up, I banged up a finger on my left (stick) hand. I figured the finger was broken and for a minute I didn't know if I would be able to play. But I stayed in and didn't give up a goal. That provided me with quite a thrill along with playing with guys like Phil and Bobby Orr, Howe and Frank Mahovlich, Jean Ratelle and Dave Keon.

I have one other memory of my first All-Star Game — an unpleasant one. Many of the players didn't put out one hundred per cent. On our bench, some of the guys poked fun at Ruel. He was giving them that old "skate, skate" bit, but they ignored him and just went through the motions. Nobody did any real hitting, either.

Maybe you could attribute this lack of incentive to the fact that the winners get only five hundred apiece. If they increased it to a thousand or fifteen hundred dollars each I think you'd see the guys flying and hitting with a little gusto. It would also produce a better game.

Two nights after the All-Star Game we played the Red Wings at Detroit. It was a big game for us. Although we had won six straight before the All-Star, we were still in fifth place, two points back of Detroit. We needed a victory to tie the Wings for fourth.

I really blew my stack in this game and was damn lucky I wasn't given at least a misconduct penalty. Pit Martin had beaten Roger Crozier twice in the opening period to give us a 2–0 lead. Now it was the second period and Gordie Howe was on the ice leading a Detroit power play.

Howe skated across the blue line and fired one of his old-fashioned wrist shots. I stopped it as I fell to my knees and trapped the puck with my pads. While I was down there waiting for the referee, Tom Smith, to whistle the play dead, Howe pushed me, the puck came loose and skidded into the net.

I went hog wild when it was ruled a goal. I threw my stick and gloves down on the ice and chased after Smith. I must have called him every curse word in the book. Stan Mikita rushed Smith, too. And while we were both yelling at Smith, Billy Reay was standing on top of our bench giving the referee the choke sign. It was a wild scene. Mikita wound up with a ten-minute misconduct penalty — I guess he can outcurse me — and I got off without even a minor penalty.

I was still fuming when I went back into the net. I think I was more furious at Howe than Smith. Gordie, you know, gets away with murder. Maybe it's because he's been a superstar for so long, but he gets away with more infractions than anybody else in the league. If it had been any other player who shoved me like that, the goal probably would have been disallowed.

We went on to win the game, though, on third-period goals by Bobby and Dennis Hull. The Canadiens snapped our seven-game winning streak in the next game, beating me, 4–1, at Montreal. I lost a tough 3–2 game to Toronto the following night, dropping us back into fifth place.

Some of us had serious doubts if we'd be able to make the playoffs. But near the end of February we started to roll again. My backup goalie now was Gerry Desjardins, an old friend from my Cleveland days. The Hawks had picked him up from Los Angeles in a trade for Denis DeJordy. I continued to play most of the games, and the pressure was getting me down. I was tired both mentally and physically.

But I got a helluva lift when I beat Detroit, 1–0, on March 26. That was my fourteenth shutout of the season and broke the NHL record set by Harry Lumley in 1954. I made a save on Frank Mahovlich in that game that I'll never forget.

The Red Wings were swarming around me during a first-period power play when I stopped a shot by Alex Delvecchio by sprawling to the right corner of the crease. The puck hit my pad and bounced to Mahovlich at the open side. Frank hesitated for a split second. I scrambled back and when he fired I slid my left leg across the goalmouth. The puck hit me on the inside of my left knee as I turned my leg sideways and bounced out.

Mahovlich was so enraged he spent the rest of the period taking stick swings at everybody's head until Doug Jarrett retaliated. Poor Frank wound up with a major penalty and we won the game on a third-period goal by Pit Martin.

Billy Reay couldn't stop talking about my save on Mahovlich after the game. "Tony," he said, "that was one of the greatest stops I've ever seen. I figured it was a sure goal until Frank hesitated and you threw that leg out."

We were now in second place, only a point back of Boston, with five games remaining. What a helluva finish was shaping up. Phil and the Bruins against me and the Black Hawks. Actually we had no games remaining against Boston, so this would be decided against common rivals.

Phil and I talked on the phone a couple of times during the

final week of the season. He was anxious for me to do well and I certainly didn't wish him any harm.

"We're going to beat you guys out of first place," Phil warned.

"That's what you think," I said. "We'll be on top when it's all over."

That final weekend was the wildest in NHL history. We went into Montreal for a Saturday night game tied with Boston for first. The tension was unbelievable. I made thirty-two saves that night and beat the Canadiens, 4–1, while the Bruins were beating the Leafs at Toronto, 4–2.

Now it was the final night of the season and we were still tied with Boston. The Bruins were playing the Leafs at Boston and we played the Canadiens at Chicago Stadium. But that afternoon a strange thing happened in New York. The Rangers bombed the Red Wings, 9–5, in a nationally-televised game. The Rangers now could beat out Montreal for the final playoff spot if the Canadiens lost to us or failed to score at least five goals.

When the Bruins, playing an hour earlier than us, beat Toronto, 3–1, everything rested on our game against Montreal. Everybody was praying. Phil and the Bruins were praying for us to lose because they wanted to finish first. The Rangers were praying for us to win because they wanted to make the playoffs. And their coach, Emile Francis, was praying for me to hold the Canadiens to less than five goals.

What an ironic situation! Emile Francis praying for me. I had heard through the grapevine earlier in the season that Francis said I was a second-rate goalie who couldn't carry Eddie Giacomin's jock. My only comment then was who the hell wants to carry Eddie's dirty old jock?

Francis must have had a fit when Yvan Cournoyer beat me to give Montreal a 1–0 lead in the first period. It was still a tight game after two periods with the Hawks leading 3–2. But when Pit Martin scored his second and third goals of the game for us early in the third period, the Canadiens were in trouble.

Claude Ruel gave up trying to win then and pulled his goalie, Rogie Vachon. He needed goals now — three of them — or his Canadiens were dead. But I wasn't about to surrender to those bastards. While I was stopping their six attackers, we got five empty net goals to win, 10–2.

What a celebration we had that night. Although we had tied Boston on total points, we were awarded first place on the strength of more victories (forty-five to forty). And I won the Vezina Trophy as the league's leading goalie.

Even Ruel found time to compliment me. "Tony beat us," he said. "He is really something. He flops all over the ice but always he stops the puck."

CHAPTER XVII

COUNTDOWN TO SHOWDOWN

Hockey fans were agog over the prospect of the Espositos facing each other in the 1970 Stanley Cup playoffs. However, some unfinished business remained. The Bruins went into the opening round of the playoffs with chips on their shoulders. Phil Esposito was carrying a chip as large as a hockey stick.

Most of us on the Bruins felt Chicago had stolen first-place money from us. Tony will disagree with me, I'm sure, but it's true, damn it.

So what if the Hawks won five more games than we did? We lost five less than they did and in the matter of tie games we had nineteen to only nine for them. And we outscored them over the season by twenty-seven goals. But we still wound up holding the dirty end of the stick.

The disappointment we felt while listening to that final Chicago-Montreal game on the radio is hard to explain. We really thought we were going to finish first. Hell, we were sure of it.

Then that damned Ruel had to pull his goaltender in the final period. I figured the Canadiens were good enough to come back from that 5–2 deficit, but Ruel obviously didn't. His move backfired on him — and the Bruins. It turned the game into a rout. No wonder Ruel isn't coaching the Canadiens anymore.

We still wound up having a great season. Bobby Orr broke all those records for a defenseman and was the leading scorer with one hundred twenty points. I finished second in the league with ninety-nine and a lot of people thought I was jealous of Bobby.

That's a lot of bull.

There have been times when I've felt I didn't get the publicity breaks Bobby got. But I've never held that against him. That would be stupid. If he has a greater appeal to the press, and the fans, so be it. He is a handsome bugger, you know, and I'm just an ugly Italian with a big nose.

The big thing that bugged me when the Hawks beat us out of first place was the way we lost it. And then there was Tony. I was happy he won the Vezina. That was a helluva accomplishment for a rookie. But like all smart-ass younger brothers, he kept rubbing it into me, especially about the Hawks finishing first. That really hurt.

When the playoffs started, I was hoping we'd get a shot at the Black Hawks eventually and show them who was boss. But first we had to get by the Rangers and the Hawks had to beat Detroit in the opening round. I didn't feel Tony would have too much trouble with the Red Wings, but I was worried about the Rangers. If any club could beat us I figured it would be those guys from New York.

Because of our higher finish, we were the hosts for the first two games against the Rangers. Harry Sinden arranged for us to stay at the Colonial Country Club in Lynnfield so we would be away from the maddening crowd. That was a laugh. I saw more Bruin fans hanging around there than you find in the lobby of Boston Garden.

On the morning of our opening playoff game, I got up at our hideaway (ha!) and had two poached eggs and toast for breakfast. Wayne Cashman, my linemate, joined me and we started talking about the Rangers.

"I suppose we'll be going against Jean Ratelle's line, eh, Cash?" I said.

"Yeah, I suppose so," Cashman said.

He looked a little uptight and so was I. This would be my seventh straight year in the playoffs and I was still nervous. I have trouble sleeping during the playoffs. I keep thinking about what we have to do to win.

Johnny Bucyk and I later broke out a deck of cards and played euchre against Johnny McKenzie and Stanfield. Bucyk and I lost. Heh, I thought, maybe that's a good sign. Unlucky at cards, lucky at hockey.

After our pre-game steak, I went back to my room for a short nap. While lying in bed I started thinking about the Rangers. Normally, I don't get mentally ready until I get to the rink.

Tony, I know, is different. He starts getting psyched up the moment he gets out of bed in the morning. Bobby Hull isn't ready until he steps on the ice.

By the time I got to Boston Garden that night, I was really "up." So were all the other guys. I don't think our club had ever been as high as we were for the Rangers that night.

Orr set the tempo on the Rangers' first rush when he smashed Dave Balon into the boards. With about four minutes gone, Hodge stole the puck from Arnie Brown and passed in front to Cashman. Cash relayed it across the goalmouth to me and Timmy Horton hit me as I slapped it behind Ed Giacomin. I was so excited I threw my hands up in the air and belted myself right in the jaw. I never even felt it, although I had a bump on my jaw after the game.

I got two other goals and Orr had a pair and we won, 8–2. Billy Speer also helped soften up the Rangers for us. He got a chance to play when Sinden decided to give Orr a rest in the third period. Billy flattened Rod Gilbert twice, Billy Fairbairn, Bob Nevin and Brad Park. He also got a good piece of Walt Tkaczuk, always a tough man to knock off his skates.

We beat the Rangers again the following night, 5–3. I got only three shots and no goals. This game stands out in my memory because the Rangers used Terry Sawchuk as their goalie instead of Giacomin. I was really surprised by this move. Giacomin has never played too well against us in Boston, but Sawchuk was then an old man and out of shape.

Sawchuk kept New York in the game until late in the second period. Then Bucyk broke a 2–2 tie by beating Terry from a tough angle and Kenny Hodge added the winner. Incidentally, that was the last game Sawchuk played. He died of injuries suffered in an altercation shortly after the playoffs.

After that second game, I warned some of our players not to get too cocky. "We have to be leery of the Rangers," I told them. "We beat them too easy. They're going to be really gunning for us in New York."

Billy Speer laughed at me and said, "Aw, we've got 'em on the run now, Phil. We'll knock 'em off in four straight." Oh, yeah. The Rangers were waiting for us just as I predicted when we showed up for the third game at Madison Square Garden. So were their fans. The people in Madison Square Garden that night were complete idiots. They got on us as soon as we skated out for our pre-game warmups. The yelling wasn't bad; you get used to that. It was the language they were using. And the insults. No man should have to take that.

Some of the banners the fans had also were filthy. I don't mean the bed sheets, but the words printed on them. They were awful. Real obscene. The fans also threw eggs at us and tomatoes and steel ball bearings. Imagine that? Ball bearings.

I knew there was going to be trouble as soon as the game started. We had heard that the Rangers were planning to get Derek Sanderson because he had played a little chippy in the first two games. And he had. That's Derek's job — to get the other guys shook up.

On Derek's first shift on the ice there was a faceoff in the circle to Giacomin's right. Giacomin left his net, skated over to Derek and said, "You'd better watch it, fella . . . we're being paid to get you tonight."

Derek, who has a quick wit, shrugged at Giacomin and said, "Hey, that's cool, man. Do your thing." Derek doesn't scare easily.

The next thing I know Derek got into a corner with Walt Tkaczuk and all hell broke loose. Three guys jumped Derek. Arnie Brown was there and then Brad Park leaped on top. On the bottom were Derek and Tkaczuk.

That's when the other guys we had on the ice went into action. Punches were flying all over the place. Park wound up fighting Dallas Smith. Don Marcotte had Tkaczuk, Derek was wrestling with Brown, Dave Balon was battling Rick Smith, and Eddie Westfall was paired against Billy Fairbairn.

John Ashley, the referee, gave Sanderson and Balon game misconducts. I couldn't believe it when Balon was thrown out of the game. It should have been Tkaczuk, who started it, or Park, who was right in the middle of it. But maybe Balon got his for continuing the fight. I don't know. What I do know is that we wound up losing the game, 4–3.

It was the roughest playoff game in history. There were twenty-four penalties called for a total of one hundred thirty-two minutes in the first period alone. All told, thirty-eight penalties were called for a total of one hundred seventy-four minutes.

Most of our guys felt Sanderson had been "suckered" by the Rangers. He agreed. "You see," Derek said, "I'm still a rookie. But I learned something tonight. They'll never pull that on me again."

Derek has changed his style of play since that game and he's a better hockey player because of it. He realized the Rangers went out there just to get him off the ice and they succeeded. They didn't plan on losing Balon, though, and that hurt them, although not as much as our loss of Sanderson.

Sinden wasn't angry at Derek, but he didn't like the idea that Emile Francis would tell his guys to 'get' Derek. And I feel Giacomin made a fool of himself. He should have kept his mouth shut and let one of his defensemen throw a challenge like that.

Wayne Cashman went out to 'get' Giacomin later in that game. He tried to hit Eddie in the head with the puck. He told him off, too. "Eddie," he said, "I'm going to cut your head off with the puck."

Cash didn't succeed with that threat, but he won two fights that night. He used some great left hooks to beat up Orland Kurtenbach, who once was regarded as the best fighter in the league, and then outslugged Fairbairn. I was surprised Cash did so well against Kurt because I had never seen Cash really go before. I think Kurt was surprised, too.

It's strange, but we were more cocky after losing that third game than we had been after the two victories in Boston. We had made it close with a pair of late goals and just missed a tie when I hit a post in the final minute. I'm sure if it had gone into overtime we would have won because we had the momentum.

Even after the Rangers won the fourth game, 4–2, to tie the series we didn't panic. This was a comparatively calm game. Cashman and Tim Horton engaged in the only real fight. Even the New York fans seemed to calm down and the Garden cops started hauling down those obscene banners.

The fifth game at Boston Garden was the best of the series — at least for us. The Rangers were leading, 2–1, late in the third period when I caught Jean Ratelle in the head with my stick. Ratty was circling in front of the New York net and I whacked at the puck, trying to knock it off his stick. He was crouched low when I stumbled. My stick shot up and creased his scalp.

Ratty brought his right glove to his head and when he removed it blood trickled down his white sweater and onto the ice. As soon as I saw the blood I mumbled, "Oh, my God, what have I done?" I knew I had caused it, but I also knew it had been an accident.

I rushed up to Ratty as he was being led off the ice and said, "It was an accident. I hope you understand that." He nodded his head and said, "Yes, I know. It was an accident."

Referee Bruce Hood gave me a five-minute major penalty. This is when the Rangers could have blown the game wide open. Earlier in the season they had scored three goals while I was sitting out a major for cutting Brad Park. But this time our penalty killers — Sanderson and Westfall, Stanfield and Marcotte and Orr — stopped the Rangers in their tracks. Then, with two minutes left on my penalty, Horton was penalized for interference. That got me off the hook.

Sitting in the dressing room between the second and third periods, most of us realized if we lost this game we were dead. That would give the Rangers the series lead and we would have to go back to New York for the next one. It would be tough beating them there.

I tied the score with a little more than two minutes gone in the third period. Cash got the puck out to me from the backboards. I reached around Ab DeMarco, the Ranger defenseman, and flipped the puck between Giacomin's right leg and the post.

The Boston fans, who had been booing us for most of the game, gave me an ovation. That made me feel good. I felt even better later in the period when I beat Giacomin again. Orr fed me a lead pass and I was all alone when I crossed the blue line. I made up my mind to shoot fast and not fool around.

Giacomin surprised me when he came out to meet me. Then he pulled up a little. That's when I let it rip. The puck flew between his pads and into the net.

Those two goals in less than six minutes put us ahead, 3–2. We protected the lead the rest of the way and went back to New York needing only one more victory to wrap up the series. When we came into Madison Square Garden for the sixth game there were the usual banners, but they were clean. One read: "We Will Bury You." Another read: "Floor Orr." But it was the Bruins who buried the Rangers and nobody buried Bobby. We could feel after the first period that the Rangers didn't have any zip left. They were beat. Orr got his first of two goals early in the second period to tie the score at 1–1. Two minutes later, Horton lost the puck to Cashman, who beat Giacomin from the left side.

Orr then finished the Rangers and almost crippled Giacomin with a shot from the right point. "Bobby kept the puck low and it hit my right boot and went in," Giacomin said later. "I could feel pain in my big toe for the rest of the game."

Some of the fans booed the Rangers when we skated off with a 4–1 victory to clinch the series. What fools. The Rangers had given us a helluva fight, even though they had to play the whole series without Vic Hadfield and Don Marshall.

We traveled back to Boston that night on a chartered plane. It was a joyous trip. Later, all of us gathered at Caruso's, a restaurant not far from my home in Salem on the north shore of Boston.

We sat there until four or five in the morning, drinking beer and talking about the playoffs. We knew we had to face the Black Hawks next. And I knew I would be facing my brother again.

The Black Hawks had earned their berth in the semifinals of the 1970 playoffs by wiping out the Detroit Red Wings in four games. The final score of each game was Chicago 4, Detroit 2 — a genuine oddity. The heroes of that series were Bobby Hull, who figured in nine goals, and Tony Esposito, who limited the Red Wings' high-scoring line of Gordie Howe, Alex Delvecchio and Frank Mahovlich to two goals. Tony, however, wasn't that impressed with his work against Detroit.

I feel we were fortunate in sweeping Detroit. This might sound strange since I gave up only eight goals in the series, but I was

Tony makes glove save in the sweep of Detroit.

just mediocre. I probably could have played better, especially in the first game. I gave up a bad goal to Howe in that one.

We were leading, 3–1, in the third period when I got careless. Delvecchio fired a shot from the left point that I stopped. Then, instead of clearing the puck to the side, or smothering it, I put it right on Howe's stick in front of the net. Gordie got clobbered by Doug Jarrett but he still managed to put the rebound past me while falling to the ice.

The Red Wings really poured it on after that and I realized if I made one more mistake the score would be tied. But Eric Nesterenko, who had set up an earlier goal by Chico Maki while killing a penalty, saved us. He put one into an empty net in the final minute.

A power play goal by Pit Martin helped us win the second game, then we moved on to Detroit for the next two. I still wasn't playing as well as I had during the regular season, but Bobby Hull was great. He won the third game almost single-handedly with two goals and two assists.

In the fourth game, Bobby set up goals by Stan Mikita and Martin and it was all over. It was the first time the Black Hawks had swept a playoff series and this, naturally, made us all feel proud.

The Red Wings didn't offer any alibis, though they could have. Frank Mahovlich had a sore left knee that bothered him throughout the series. And I know Howe had lung congestion caused by a bad cold, and his left wrist was aching.

I have all the respect in the world for guys like Howe and Mahovlich. They really impressed me the way they continued to play even though they weren't in top shape.

When Mahovlich did get on the ice, Nesterenko did a great job tying him up. And Martin covered Garry Unger like a blanket. Unger didn't score a single goal in the series after getting forty-two during the regular season.

While we were celebrating our clean sweep of Detroit, Bobby Hull offered a warning that was ignored by most of us. He wondered first how long it would take the Bruins and the Rangers to decide their series. "A layoff now might not be the best thing in the world for us," Bobby said. "We might lose our edge."

I welcomed the rest. I had been under a lot of pressure for weeks and I was whipped. So I sat around our apartment in Chicago, taking it easy and rooting for Phil and the Bruins. When the Bruins finally eliminated the Rangers, I was happy for Phil . . . and a little apprehensive, too.

Now the stage was set for a real family showdown.

CHAPTER XVIII

CHAMPAGNE FROM THE CUP

The head-on meeting between the Espositos in the 1970 Stanley Cup playoffs captured the imagination of sport fans because of its uniqueness. For the first time in 41 years, a player found himself shooting pucks at his brother in the playoffs. Only those with long memories were able to recall a similar confrontation. It happened in the 1929 playoffs when the Boston Bruins beat the New York Rangers in the championship series. The Boston goalie was Cecil (Tiny) Thompson; his brother Paul was a forward for the Rangers.

Considering the historical significance, there was tremendous pressure on the Espositos when they faced each other in the opening game of the Chicago-Boston playoff series at Chicago Stadium on Sunday afternoon, April 19, 1970. Phil remembers.

I scored three goals against Tony that day and we won, 6–3. But Tony had an excuse for giving up six goals. A shot by Ken Hodge in the opening minutes struck him high on his mask above the left eye. If he hadn't been wearing the mask he may have been killed.

Here's how it happened:

I was on the ice with my linemates, Hodge and Wayne Cashman. We worked the puck deep into the Chicago zone. Hodge wound up with it near the baseline to Tony's left and, using Pit Martin as a screen, he let go a wicked slap shot. Tony never saw it.

When the puck banged off Tony's mask, he fell to the ice and

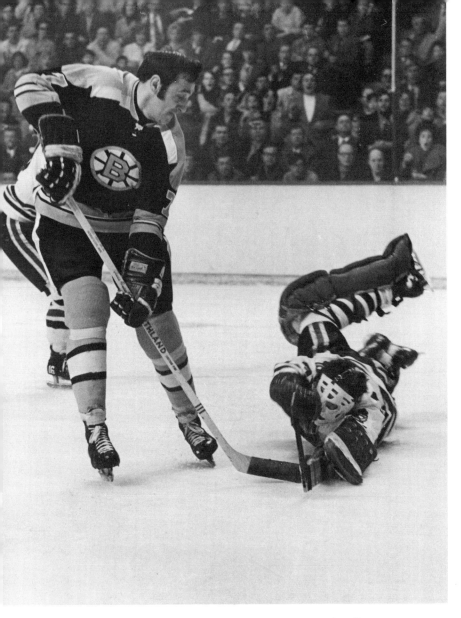

Phil gives Tony a rough time in the opening game of playoff series.

lay there motionless. "God," I mumbled to myself, "I hope he's not seriously hurt." I had seen our goalie, Ed Johnston, get hit in the head in a practice earlier in the season. Eddie spent seven or eight weeks in the hospital and it was feared he might need brain surgery. He didn't, but it was a scary accident.

Now, as Tony lay face down on the ice, I was really concerned. I wanted to go to him, but instead I remained near center ice, skating around in circles and praying. I kept glancing over my shoulder at him. Bobby Hull eventually came to me and said, "He's a little dazed, but he seems all right, Phil." Bobby then attempted to inject a little humor into the situation. "It hit Tony in the head, so he should be okay," he said. "You Espositos have hard heads."

Bobby was right. Tony and I do have hard heads. I tried to smile at Bobby but couldn't. I was still worried even after Tony got to his feet. He looked a little wobbly. I think Billy Reay made a mistake then. He should have pulled Tony out of the game.

After taking another few minutes to shake the cobwebs out of his head, Tony went back into the net. He wasn't as sharp as he could have been. Obviously, that shot in the head was paining him.

I scored my first two goals off him in the opening period. On the first, Hodge gave me the puck in front of the net. I had it on my backhand and Tony must have figured I was going to pass off to John Bucyk on my left. I got good wood on the shot. The puck hit a post, caromed off Tony's chest and dropped in.

Just before the end of the period, the Hawks were killing a penalty to Doug Jarrett when I took a pass from Bobby Orr. This time I kept the puck low and slid it under Tony.

Lucky me. I had scored only two goals off Tony during the entire regular season. Now I had beaten him twice in one period. The Hawks seemed to let up after that and my third goal in the second period, which was a little flukey, just about finished them.

I was unable to see Tony after the game. I recall somebody came into our locker room and said, "Tony has a nasty bruise on the left forehead."

This worried me. "Has he gone to the hospital?" I asked. "Tell him to get that checked. Remember when Eddie Johnston got hit like that. Tell Tony he'd better get to a hospital."

Tony Esposito didn't bother going to the hospital that day. The injury was only a minor one. What was aching him more after the game was the damage to his pride.

I was aggravated at myself and not at Phil or Ken Hodge after the game. That week off — while waiting for the Bruins to eliminate the Rangers — actually hindered me. I think the more I play the better I play. And when I'm not playing steadily, I get rusty.

Instead of working hard in practice, I took it easy trying to conserve my energy. This was stupid. I thought the team played well enough in the first game, but I didn't do my job. I was terrible.

Hodge's shot stung when it hit me. He really blasted it. I was stunned all right, but after going to the bench and taking smelling salts, I figured I was okay. A goalie has to worry about being puck shy after being hit like that because you're bound to be shaky. That's why I went back into the net — to test myself.

Maybe I was fighting the puck a little bit after that. This can happen. It has happened to me even when I haven't been hit during a game and I have yet to figure out why. You struggle to avoid giving up a bad goal and you find yourself fighting the puck, juggling it instead of holding it or missing it completely when you try to glove it.

The best example was Phil's third goal in that opening game. I failed to clear a rebound and Phil was there to grab it. He whacked it and the puck went up at an angle. I was just getting up from my knees and I reached for it and it went off the end of my glove into the net.

My reflexes weren't good on that one. I was maybe a half-second behind and it cost me. That whole game caused me a lot of misery. It was the first time I remember the Chicago fans booing me. And maybe I deserved it. I just didn't do the job.

Billy Reay wasn't too happy with the result either. "I think our guys have been too busy reading their clippings," he told one reporter. "They sat around for a week listening to people tell them how great they were and it was natural for them to start believing it. But I think they learned they're not quite that great."

The coach was right. We had goofed off a little in the first game and we weren't much better the following night. I know I didn't play well and we lost, 4–1.

Bobby Orr scored a goal, his first one of the season against me. It was in the first period on a breakaway. I came out of the net to charge him and he got the puck over me. It was my own fault. I should have stayed in the net and made him make the first move. Phil got the Bruins' clinching goal. He's always there, you know. He's the toughest man for a defenseman to move out from in front of the net. This is one of his biggest assets. He beat me from close range with a good shot. That gave him four goals in two games against me. Geez, he was hot.

When the series moved to Boston for the third and fourth games I was beginning to wonder if we would win a game. Bobby Hull hadn't scored a goal in the series. Eddie Westfall was covering him and doing a helluva job. And Stan Mikita was having his share of troubles, too.

Phil and I talked on the phone only once. He wanted to visit with us when the Bruins were in Chicago and see Mark Anthony, his godchild, but he decided against it. This was the playoffs. It was strictly business now.

Phil got another goal off me in the third game and John Bucyk got two and the Bruins won, 5–2. Bucyk made me look terrible. He's a real opportunist. He's always in the right spot and he doesn't waste any energy. I call him "Old Lurk." He hides around the corner, gets the puck, bang, and it's in.

I suppose when you get to be a vet like John you know where to be all the time — and I mean all the time. He's tough in the corners and he's got a good shot. He never shoots for the same spot. Give him an opening and he goes for it. He shoots for the top corner or the low corner or slides it along the ice so you never know where he's aiming.

In that third game, we were leading, 2–1, early in the second period when Keith Magnuson was penalized for offensive inter-ference — a bad call. Then came the Boston power play, led by Phil and Bucyk. John got the puck to my right and just outside the crease. He cut loose with a backhander and the puck skipped through my legs. Old Lurk is a dirty bugger.

Phil set up Bucyk's second power play goal later in the period. That was the one that killed us. Magnuson again was in the penalty box for holding Orr. Phil took Orr's pass out in the faceoff circle to my left. When I moved to cover Phil, he passed to Bucyk at the opposite corner. John had the entire right side to shoot at and he didn't miss.

That loss really put us behind the eight-ball. One more and it would be all over. The fourth game was nationally televised on a Sunday afternoon from Boston Garden. I wanted to go to Mass that day. I'm not the most religious man in the world, but I always feel better after going to church. This day, though, I missed Mass. I was tired and worried, and I overslept.

It was a warm spring day and most of us were sweating when we showed up at the Garden and started to dress. I was sweating most of all. The pressure was really getting to me and I remember telling one of our guys that I was exhausted.

"I don't know how long I'm going to be able to hang in there today," I said.

Bobby Hull heard me moaning and said, "Tony, just give it your best. And try to relax."

In the Bruins' dressing room all was serene. The scene, as Phil re-creates it, was a happy one, with twenty carefree players exchanging wise cracks as they got into their work clothes.

We were real loosey-goosey. There was no tension like we experienced before every New York game. Being three games up, we knew there was no way we were going to lose.

Although Tony and I had not communicated with each other, aside from a phone call, I knew he must have been downhearted. He had been playing well, but we had been bombarding him with shots in every game. This was strictly business, as he has so often said, but I couldn't help feeling sorry for him.

Maybe, I decided, the trouble with the Black Hawks was their lack of experience. They had so many rookies on that team. And the vets among them had been having a tough series. Bobby Hull still was looking for his first goal. And Stan Mikita looked bad.

He wasn't skating.

Gerry Cheevers, meanwhile, had been playing great goal for us. He had given up only six goals in the first three games. Cheesy had never looked better. As he sat across from me in the dressing room, I could see he was brimming with confidence. So were the other guys.

Before we went out on the Garden ice, somebody yelled, "Okay, guys, let's wrap it up."

I yelled back, "Yeah, the Hawks are dead. Let's bury 'em."

But we soon found out that the Hawks weren't dead. Bobby Hull was flying again and so was Mikita. And when Dennis Hull scored twice in less than four minutes in the second period to put Chicago ahead, 3–2, I wondered if maybe we hadn't been a little overconfident. They were outplaying us and we were struggling.

Tony was fantastic in that second period. We took twenty-two shots at him — that amounted to more than a shot a minute — and he missed only one. Freddy Stanfield beat him with a forty-footer that tied the score at 3–3.

Bryan Campbell put the Hawks ahead again when he scored during a power play early in the third period. By now Tony looked dead tired. He interrupted play once and went to the Chicago bench for a sip of water. When he took off his mask I could see his face was beet-red. The heat and the pressure must have been unbearable.

With about seven minutes left, both Mikita and Cliff Koroll missed poke checks on Wayne Cashman at the blue line. Cash passed to me and flipped the puck in the direction of the net. Hodge, standing there alone, tipped it in to tie the score at 4–4.

The Garden crowd went wild over that one. I was thinking we would have to decide this one in overtime when Johnny McKenzie intercepted Mikita's clearing pass with less than two minutes to play. Pie passed to Stanfield and Fred gave him a quick return pass. McKenzie started to cut in from right wing. In this situation, Pie always waits to see if the goalie will drop his left shoulder. That's exactly what Tony did and Pie's shot flew over his shoulder and hit high in the net.

As McKenzie skated around the back of the net, his arms outstretched, Tony dropped to his knees, a picture of dejection. You knew he was ready to cry right there And I swear you could see his look of agony right through the mask.

I was overjoyed at sweeping the Hawks, my old team, but I got upset in the dressing room when Derek Sanderson insulted my brother. I had just finished telling a reporter how proud I was of Tony when Derek interrupted our conversation.

"Aw, your brother's a cocky bastard," Derek said, "and he's not really that great a goalie."

I suppose he was just trying to pull my leg, but I was ready to choke Derek.

"You've been bugging me about Tony all year," I said. "Now get the hell out of here and stop bothering me."

Derek walked away and I was glad of that. I didn't want to continue arguing with him in front of the reporters. And, besides, I was worrying about Tony now and how he had accepted the defeat.

Defeat has always been hard for Tony Esposito
to accept. He accepted this one, but not the remarks
made by Sanderson.

When I heard that Sanderson had called me a cocky bastard after that game, I almost choked. Of all people. If anybody is cocky, it's that flippin' Derek. But maybe it's something you have to expect from him.

He's a pretty fair hockey player, not a star, and this is his way of fighting his way into the limelight — by mouthing off. When Derek grew his mustache, a lot of guys in the league made fun of him. I couldn't care less. Let him grow a beard and go all the way.

It's his remarks that get under my skin. I have never put the rap on anybody in the league. But there are always a few guys who enjoy cutting up others. This should be stopped. They only prove how illiterate and immature they are.

Derek and I have had a few words on the ice. And sometimes it has gone beyond words. One time I was trying to clear the puck and he elbowed me and we had a little tussle. Off the ice, though, he has treated me pretty well and that's fine because otherwise I'd bust him in the mustache.

He also seems to have changed his opinion of me as a goalie. He admits now that I'm better than he gave me credit for. I just

It was all over for the disconsolate Tony.

wish he had said that after the 1970 playoffs because that's when I needed encouragement.

I was completely exhausted when I got to the visiting team's locker room after the final game against the Bruins. The Bruins had thrown fifty-four shots at me. I had no stamina left when McKenzie scored the winning goal. Hell, I couldn't even raise my arm.

I remember McKenzie cutting in from the right side and then Bucyk moved in front of the net, blocking my view. I didn't see the puck. I went low and prayed. But when I heard that roar from the Boston crowd I didn't have to look for the puck. I knew it was in the net.

So it was all over for the Black Hawks. We shook hands with the Bruins. They deserved to win. Then I saw Phil and wished him luck in the finals.

It had been twelve years since the Bruins had reached the Stanley Cup final round. They had a week off waiting for their opponent to be determined. When the St. Louis Blues finally eliminated the Pittsburgh Penguins, the Bruins were ready, according to Phil.

We didn't allow ourselves to get rusty as the Hawks had done. When we flew out to St. Louis for the series opener we figured we had too much power for the Blues. The only game we were concerned about was the first. We were aware that St. Louis had never beaten an Eastern Division team in the playoffs. If we won that first one on their home ice, it would give us a big psychological edge.

We won it, 6–1, without even breaking a sweat. John Bucyk played the best game I ever saw him play. Chief was fantastic. He scored three goals and just missed a couple more.

The score was tied at 1–1 in the second period when Jacques Plante, who was then the Blues' goalie, suffered an injury that knocked him out of the game and the playoffs. Freddy Stanfield shot the puck and I deflected it. It hit the handle of my stick and flew up, catching Plante high on his mask and knocking him unconscious.

"Here we go again," I thought. It was similar to the Hodge shot that Tony had stopped with his mask in our opening game against Chicago. But this one was more severe. It cracked Plante's mask and put him in the hospital with a concussion. Imagine what would have happened to poor Jake if he hadn't been wearing the mask?

The Blues claimed that was the turning point of the game — and the series. I'm not so sure about that. Ernie Wakely took over for Plante and gave up five goals to us. But I feel we would have won that game if St. Louis had two men in the net. We outplayed the Blues by even more than the score indicated. We were all over them.

Scotty Bowman, then Blues' coach, surprised a lot of people by putting Jimmy Roberts on Orr. That was real funny. Every time Bobby came on the ice, Scotty would send out Roberts and tell him to shadow Bobby and forget everybody else. I never understood Scotty's reasoning. How could he waste one guy from his attack to cover a defenseman? He was giving up too much. Now Roberts is a pretty good checker, but Bobby left him standing still so many times it was unreal.

Harry Sinden thought it was funny, too. He said, "Let Roberts watch Bobby, I don't care. I don't think one man can cover Bobby anyway, so let him watch. That way it will leave our forwards open." Harry was right. While Roberts was shadowing Orr, our forwards, especially Bucyk, went wild. And Bobby still managed to set up a goal by Sanderson in that game. That really rubbed it into the Blues and Roberts and Bowman.

Our next two games were laughers, too. We beat Wakely, 6–2, in the second game with Eddie Westfall and Sanderson getting two goals apiece. In the third game, Glenn Hall took over as the Blues' goaltender. That old bugger was great that night, but we still wound up beating him, 4–1. It was our ninth straight victory, all with Cheevers in the net.

We were already celebrating the championship by now. In our rooms at the Colonial Country Club we joked around a lot and guzzled beer which you normally don't do because you're worried about how you're going to feel the next day. But we had nothing to worry about.

On the day of the fourth game — it was Sunday, May 10 — most of the guys were getting ready to go to Boston Garden in our chartered bus when Sinden approached us.

"If you guys want to take your cars in it's okay," Harry said. "Then if we wrap it up today you can drive right back here to the Colonial and we'll have a helluva party."

I drove into the Garden in Bucyk's car. Orr and McKenzie were with us. We walked around in the dressing room shouting, "Let's win it . . . yeah, let's win it and get to the party." Sanderson showed up with a tuxedo. He said he wanted to be dressed in style for the party.

That fourth game, though, started out differently. The Blues were different. They were really up for the game. I scored in the second period to tie the score at 2–2. It was my thirteenth goal of the playoffs and wiped out the league record shared by Rocket Richard and Jean Beliveau, two pretty fair hockey players.

But the Blues didn't quit. They went ahead early in the third period on a goal by Larry Keenan. Then Bucyk, the old war horse, scored with less than seven minutes left to send the game into overtime.

Before we went out for the start of the "sudden death" period, Sinden told us to "shoot the works and don't hold back." He decided to go with Sanderson on the faceoff, keeping me on the bench. It worked out great when Derek and Orr combined for a picture play.

Keenan was trying to clear the puck off the boards in the St. Louis end when Bobby took an awful chance. He moved in from his right point position to block the clearing pass. If he had missed it he would have been caught out of position. But Bobby is so quick and has such great anticipation he intercepted the puck and passed to Derek, who headed for the net and then passed it back to Bobby.

As Bobby cut in front of the St. Louis net, Noel Picard tripped him. But Bobby still whipped the puck past Glenn Hall, then went flying through the air, making a three-point landing to the right of the net.

Bobby Orr, that wonderful kid, had won it for us after only

forty seconds of overtime. The Bruins, for the first time in twenty-nine years, were the Stanley Cup champions.

I almost injured myself trying to rush onto the ice to congratulate Bobby. No kidding. As the other guys jumped over the boards, the bench went flying and I fell flat on my face. By the time I reached Bobby, he was at the bottom of a pile of players.

Later, as we were gathered at center ice and the NHL president, Clarence Campbell, presented the cup to Bucyk, somebody said, "Let's get Greenie. He ought to be in on this." Teddy Green was standing back in the crowd, tears running down his face.

Bobby and I escorted him out on the ice. Now Teddy was really weeping and it made me feel a little sad. If he hadn't suffered that head injury in training camp he wouldn't have been a spectator on this great day. He would have been out there with us, helping to beat the Blues.

In our dressing room there was complete bedlam. We slugged down some of the champagne and beer but poured most of it over our heads like raving maniacs. Then we started tossing people into the shower, including some of the fathers who wandered in. Orr's dad got the treatment and so did Stanfield's dad. Somebody yelled, "Let's get your old man, Phil."

I said, "Sure, why not. But who's going to pick up the big bugger?" Hodge and Carleton, our two biggest players, volunteered for the mission, but couldn't find my dad. It turned out he was the smart one of the bunch. He was in a nearby room, sipping champagne with the wives.

The party we had later that night at the Colonial was really something. Cheevers and I grabbed the microphone and led the singing. But nothing compared to the victory parade we had through downtown Boston two days later. It was the most fantastic, scary thing I have ever been in.

I don't think anybody anticipated such madness. For one thing, they didn't have enough cops along the parade route to control the people. I rode in a car with Bucyk, Westfall and Green. The people were yelling and grabbing at us. I had my tie ripped off and was almost strangled. And I wound up with a torn finger from people trying to grab my championship ring.

When we got to City Hall, Sanderson and Orr told me the

damndest story of all. They said at one point in the parade, one girl took off her clothes and showed everything. Now how in hell did I miss that?

But the Bruins' fans had every right to run amok. They had waited a long time to get that Stanley Cup back to Boston. And I was happy to be a part of such a wild and wonderful celebration.

CHAPTER XIX

TOGETHER IN DEFEAT

Intense rivals on the ice, the Espositos spend most of their summers together — running hockey schools, playing softball, and drinking beer at family barbecues on Lake Superior. That was how they enjoyed the summer after the Bruins won the Cup. Then it was time for the start of another season of hockey. Phil was anxious to get to the Bruins' training camp to meet a new coach and renew acquaintances with an old friend.

Harry Sinden shocked many people by quitting as the Bruins' coach just three days after we had won the Stanley Cup. I wasn't too surprised because midway through the 1969-70 season Harry had told me he was upset with the way things were being run behind his back. I assumed then he was having trouble with the front office.

The newspapers claimed Sinden quit because the Bruins refused to give him a decent raise. He was making between twenty and twenty-two thousand dollars a year, which is peanuts for a major-league coach these days. But money wasn't the only reason he decided to turn his back on the Bruins and go into the home construction business in upstate New York. Harry's family was growing up and he wanted to spend more time with his wife and four daughters.

I was sorry to see Harry leave the club. But I was happy when Tom Johnson was named as his successor. Tommy has always treated me great. Harry did, too, but he has a different personality. I found it harder to discuss things with Harry. He had his little "in" jokes

In the summer the brothers teach hockey at their school.

with other guys on the club which I didn't always understand. With Tommy, I participate more in his jokes because I dig him. Some of the players don't and I guess some of them feel like outsiders now — the way I did with Harry.

Johnson, of course, was no stranger to the club or to the players when he took charge at our training camp in London, Ontario. He had been in the Bruins' organization since 1963, first as a player and then as an assistant to general manager Milt Schmidt. Tommy had never coached a team before, but he showed good sense right off the bat.

At one of our first meetings at camp he said, "Look, guys, I'm going to give you free rein here. You've got four weeks to get in shape. Make sure you do because otherwise you'll be in trouble."

That's what I mean by good sense. Tommy had been an All-Star defenseman with Montreal before coming to Boston. He had gone through many of these training camp grinds, so he knew the score. He accepted the fact we were the defending champs and treated us accordingly.

There were mixed emotions among the players when Johnson took over. Some liked him, some didn't. Eventually, though, everybody came to respect Tom.

Most of the talk in camp centered around the return of Teddy Green. He had missed a whole season because of the fractured skull he suffered a year earlier. It was good to see Greenie in uniform again. Still, we wondered if he would be able to skate and do the things he did before the accident when he was one of the league's top defensemen.

At our first practice, everybody was standing around, waiting for Teddy to come out. This would be a big moment for him. When Teddy finally joined us on the ice he started skating slowly at first, then gradually picked up steam. He really surprised me.

"Greenie," I said, "you look better skating now than you did before the accident."

He appreciated that. "I feel terrific," he said.

So did I. I had checked into camp at two hundred seventeen pounds, which is about seven over my best playing weight. But this didn't worry me. I knew it wouldn't take me long to get into shape.

Hockey training camps are too long anyway. I don't think you need four weeks. It's just not necessary. If a player stays reasonably fit during the off-season he should be ready to play in two weeks. But management prolongs the training period to get in ten exhibition games and pick up a few extra bucks.

I always pace myself at camp. I don't work hard — at least during the first week because I don't want to pull a muscle and miss the start of the season. I get myself in half-decent shape and apply a little pressure in the exhibition games. Then when they drop the puck for the opening game of the regular season, I'm ready.

I was ready when we opened the 1970-71 season against Detroit at Boston Garden. I got a goal in the first five minutes and we won, 7–3. It was the start of something big, although I didn't realize it at the time.

Our second home game was against the Black Hawks. Tony, that sonofagun, stopped me cold and we were lucky to get a 3–3 tie. Greenie got the first goal of his comeback in our next game at Boston Garden. It was against the Philadelphia Flyers.

Ken Hodge had the puck in the corner and passed it out to me. I shot, Bernie Parent stopped it and Greenie moved in fast and whacked in the rebound. The Garden fans went wild. They were on their feet, yelling and screaming for Teddy. When I skated over to congratulate him, tears were running down Greenie's cheek. He was very moved by the standing ovation, and so was I.

It was one helluva thing to see Teddy get that first goal. He was starting to come around by then. At first his reflexes were a little slow. His timing was off and consequently he would lose the puck on occasions and this destroyed his confidence. But that goal against the Flyers provided him with a big lift. It gave the whole team a big lift.

We were unbeaten in thirty straight home games when we ran into Glenn Hall of the St. Louis Blues one night early in November. He beat us, 2–0. Glenn was as good that night as I've ever seen him. I think I had ten or eleven shots myself and couldn't fool him.

But that was only a temporary setback for us. We bounced back to beat the Canadiens, 6–1, at the Garden the following weekend. After that game I remember kidding around with my linemates, Hodge and Wayne Cashman. We were real loose.

"Hey," I said, "we got a line this year that can really fly."
Hodgie laughed and said, "Yeah, Phil, let's keep flying."
And we did. After only thirteen games our line had nineteen goals. I had nine of them. After twenty-six games — which was one-third of the season — I had twenty-two goals and forty-nine points. A writer from *The Sporting News* approached me then and reminded me that at that pace I would end up with sixty-six goals. "There's no way I'm going to score sixty-six," I told him. I wasn't putting him on, either.

Even when we reached the All-Star Game break in January my thoughts weren't on any records. I had forty-two goals and eighty-seven points then. I figured it would be nice to get one hundred points for the third straight season and I wanted our team to finish first in the standings. The Bruins hadn't done that in thirty years. But I wasn't thinking of records.

The first half of the 1970-71 season consisted mainly of trouble and toil for Tony Esposito. The trouble started with his contract negotiations with Tommy Ivan, the general manager of the Black Hawks. The toil followed.

Tommy Ivan is from the old school of front office hockey men. He's a tough negotiator. The first contract he offered me during the summer of 1970 was ridiculous. He was going to give me a pay raise of five hundred dollars. Imagine that!

I had been named the Rookie of the Year in the National Hockey League and had won the Vezina Trophy as the league's top goalie and Tommy Ivan was offering me five hundred more than I had made the previous season.

After recovering from that shock I wrote Ivan a letter and told him I couldn't accept his ridiculous offer. That was in August, and when I didn't hear anything from Ivan I phoned Alan Eagleson, the head of the NHL Players Association, and asked for his advice.

Eagleson listened to the contract terms Ivan had offered and told me I wouldn't be making nearly as much as most of the goalies in the league.

"That's what's bugging me," I said. "I figure I should be one

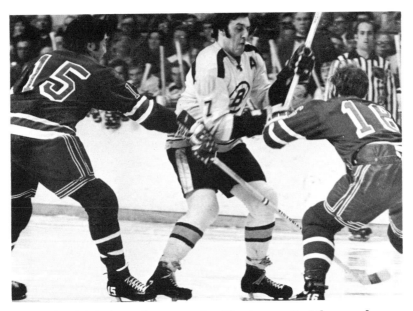

Phil didn't always have smooth sailing in pursuit of the record.

All Stars: Phil, Bobby Hull, Gordie Howe, Brad Park and Bobby Orr.

of the highest paid goalies. But I don't want to let it ride until training camp. I'd like to resolve the whole thing before then. Otherwise, I won't feel obliged to report to camp."

Eagleson said not to worry, that he would talk to Ivan and straighten everything out. But now it was getting close to the opening of camp and nothing was settled and I was concerned. The newspapers had picked it up and the publicity was mostly bad for me. So I called Alan again and asked what I should do.

"You better get to camp and we'll try to settle the whole thing there," he said.

"Okay, I'll go to camp," I said.

When I got to the Hawks' camp at St. Catherines, Ontario, Ivan played it real cool. I had several talks with him over a span of a couple of weeks and played in the exhibition games. I didn't work as hard as I could because I was worried about getting injured. Sure enough, I did get hurt. I got hit with pucks a couple of times and once I needed five stitches for a cut beneath the chin.

In one of those exhibition games we were playing the Bruins and Phil beat me with a great move. He was out killing a penalty when he picked up a loose puck, skated between Pat Stapleton and Bill White, and broke in alone. I moved out to cut down on his angle, but he faked me out and put it in the net.

Phil then skated back through the crease, poked me with his stick and said, "You know better than to rush the star of the family."

That's Phil. Always the kidder.

I wasn't in a kidding mood, though, because I still had my contract on my mind and it was nerve-wracking. I had several more talks with Ivan and Eagleson and we finally worked out an agreement. I signed a three-year contract for six figures. That was the base pay, but it also included performance bonuses and escalation clauses. I was reasonably happy with it because now I wouldn't have to argue over contracts for three years, and I'm sure they were happy, too.

For the remainder of the exhibition games I was just mediocre. Not too good and not too bad. I was the same when the regular season started. I simply wasn't playing up to my potential. Maybe it was a lack of concentration. After the rookie year I had, the fans in Chicago expected me to produce again. They had dubbed me as being great, and this can make a man think he is better than he really is. So I felt a lot of pressure at the start of the season. Our entire team seemed a little lax in those early games. We were winning but not playing as well as we could have played. This was the first season the Black Hawks played in the Western Division and the early schedule was a piece of cake. For instance, only three of our first twelve home games were against the established teams.

We lost only three of our first seventeen games. All three losses were charged to me while Gerry Desjardins, my backup man, was unbeaten in his first five games. Gerry was playing great. However, he was being spotted by Billy Reay so that I was playing against all the tougher teams and he was saved for the weaker teams.

Reay apparently didn't have too much confidence in Gerry, although he started using him against the tougher clubs as the season went along. Gerry and I are rivals in a sense. What I mean is we like to see each other do well and we root for each other, but there is still pressure involved. If I have a good game, he's got added pressure on him to produce in the next game and vice-versa.

This is all part of big-league hockey, of course, and it does help keep us both sharp. The mental strain, though, is always there. I go into games so shook up some times that it's almost unbearable. I know what I'm supposed to do, but I can barely think straight. I'm so involved in the game I don't see the fans or hear them.

There are other goalies who refuse to get that worked up and I envy them. They claim they play better if they're not worried and shaky. I guess it's a difference in temperament. Before a game I don't concern myself with anything but getting ready. And if my hands are trembling a little bit, all the better. That's when I play my best.

The only advice I would offer a young goaltender with dreams of playing in the NHL some day is to prepare yourself for each game in the same way. Be ready. Be alert. And if you find it hard to relax before a game, don't worry about it. Most of us pros feel the same pressures. The important thing is to be on your toes once the game starts. If you're not fully prepared, the other team is going to sense it and put pressure on you and score some goals.

There is nothing to compare with the mental strain I go through when I'm getting ready for a game against Phil and the Bruins. I remember a game in early December during the 1970-71 season when I beat the Bruins, 4–3. Phil got all three Boston goals.

I was happy we had won but furious at Phil for beating me three times. On one of his goals he got the puck in front of the net and waited for me to make a move and then fired it into the net before I had a chance to react. A few days later I got a letter from a lady in Waukegan, Illinois, who claimed I should never be allowed to play against my brother because I don't try to stop him. Some fans are so stupid.

How do you stop a guy like Phil? He's got everything going for him. He's got size and strength. He can shoot, he can stick-handle, he can check. He's the best around. And you don't have to ask the so-called experts for their opinion. By this I mean the reporters. They're supposed to be the experts, but what do they know? Most of them never played a game of hockey in their lives.

Instead, just talk to some other hockey players about Phil. They'll tell you he's almost impossible to stop once he gets the puck and lets it go.

After that game against Boston, Derek Sanderson of the Bruins paid me quite a compliment. He was quoted as saying, "We should have won and didn't. And do you know who made the difference out there? Tony Esposito. He's now one of the best goalies around. I didn't think so when he first broke in. I figured he was a fluke. But now I put him right up there with Ed Giacomin of the Rangers."

I appreciated those kind words from Derek, but I was still having my share of troubles as mid-season approached. I had suffered a broken bone in the ring finger of my right hand early in January. Since I'm a southpaw, the right is my catching hand. I had to sit out four games and then came back with the finger still aching me. I had a piece of fiber taped in the pocket of my trapper glove. I couldn't close it, so the puck used to hit the trapper and bounce out.

This affected my play a little and I had to make adjustments in my style of playing the puck. Since I couldn't catch shots fired at my glove side, I would bat them down and then fall on the puck in the crease.

The finger continued to give me trouble but my average remained respectable. It was 2.25 at mid-season when I was named to the West team for the annual All-Star Game at Boston. That meant I would be playing against Phil in his own rink, the Boston Garden.

Our parents came to Boston for the game. Mom, who refuses to watch Phil and I play against each other, wouldn't leave Phil's house. But dad was there in all his glory. Before the game he predicted the West would win, 2–1. He hit it right on the button.

It was a big night for the Black Hawks. Bobby Hull and Chico Maki scored the West's goals and I played fairly well. At least Phil didn't beat me. I did give up a goal to Yvan Cournoyer in the first period, but that was it. Ernie Wakely of St. Louis relieved me midway in the game and held the East scoreless the rest of the way.

I feel we won that game — it was the first time the West beat the East — because we were hungrier. The East guys acted like fat cats. One of the fattest was Brad Park of the Rangers. He skated up to Dennis Hull before the game and said, "Do you guys really think you have a chance tonight?"

Park thinks he's a prima donna, you know, and his remark aggravated me. He was acting as if we had a lot of nerve just showing up for the game. But I think we showed him something before it was over. To me, it's a great honor just being named to the All-Star team.

Phil doesn't share his brother's enthusiasm for All-Star games, mainly because of the small purses at stake.

Those games are a complete, hopeless farce. Imagine awarding only five hundred dollars to each member of the winning team. Are they kidding? And the losers get only three hundred fifty apiece. Hell, after Tony beat us in the 1971 game my check after taxes was one hundred fifty-two dollars. At that time I was getting paid four times that for each game during the regular season.

The fans figure we should go out there and work our butts off to win the All-Star Game. Sure, you should try to win for the pride and prestige involved, but if you get hurt in that game nobody is going to give a damn about you. You're finished. You might get your salary for the rest of the season, but what do you do if it's a permanent injury? You wind up selling beer for a living. I never work too hard in an All-Star Game and I never will until they raise the ante. It should be conducted like the pro football All-Star Game where they give two thousand dollars to each guy on the winning team and fifteen hundred apiece to the losers. Then you'd really see a hockey game because the guys would be trying.

Before that 1971 game, Tom Johnson had a chat with the Bruins who were on the East team. He said, "Look, I want you guys to try, but be damn careful you don't get hurt." He then reminded us that Bobby Orr banged up a knee in one of his first All-Star games and it took him a long time to get over it.

So Tony figured the West won because his teammates were hungrier, and he was right. I'll never be that hungry as long as they insist on giving us such lousy purses.

I took that loss in the All-Star Game in stride and got a chuckle out of my dad picking the right score. At the time he was also picking the Bruins to win the Eastern Division championship. I hoped he was right. The Rangers then were giving us a good battle for first. But we started to open up ground on them early in February and just about finished them in a game at Boston Garden on February 9 when we beat New York, 6–3. That gave us a nine-point lead.

It wasn't until then that I started to think about records. I had forty-seven goals and one hundred six points in fifty-three games. That meant I had twenty-five games left to break Bobby Hull's record of fifty-eight goals in one season and my own league record of one hundred twenty-six points.

I broke both records in a game against the Kings in Los Angeles on March 11. That afternoon Derek Sanderson and I went to a Hollywood film studio and were introduced to Paul Anka and Shirley Bassey. Paul, who is quite a hockey fan, asked me, "Are you going to break the record tonight, Phil?" I replied, "Well, if I get lucky I might."

The previous night at Oakland, I had tied Bobby's record with my fifty-eighth goal, but I had another goal nullified by a tripping penalty to Wayne Cashman. I also hit a couple of posts with shots that should have gone in. In the first period against the Kings, I hit another post and I mumbled to myself, "Oh, God, here we go again."

But my luck changed later in the first period. I was stationed in front of Los Angeles goalie Denis DeJordy, and Gilles Marotte, the Kings' defenseman, was trying to move me out when Teddy Green fired a shot from the point. I slid off Marotte, moved back toward the slot and tipped Teddy's shot between DeJordy's legs. All the guys jumped off our bench and came out to congratulate me on the record. It was quite a thrill. I picked up my one hundred twenty-seventh point to break my own league record when I assisted on a goal by John Bucyk late in the first period and added my sixtieth goal in the second period. That was another lucky goal. Dallas Smith's shot bounced off the boards to me, I trapped it, pulled DeJordy out of the net and tucked it in.

The only thing I regretted was that I had broken the records on the road — more than three thousand miles from Boston. But there were almost three hundred Bruin fans there in the Forum. They had made the trip out to the West Coast on one of those package deals for vacationers. They gave me a standing ovation after each goal and so did even some of the Los Angeles fans.

We won that game, 7–2. It was our sixty-seventh game of the season, so I had eleven games to add to the records. Maybe I can get sixty-six, I told myself. I passed that mark in a game against Buffalo on March 21, the night after we clinched the pennant at Philadelphia.

Then Tom Johnson started to rest some of us regulars for the playoffs and we went into a tailspin, losing four straight games. But we bounced back to win our final three games of the regular season.

In our final regular-season game at Boston Garden we beat the Canadiens, 7–2. I got my seventh hat trick, another single season record, and wound up with seventy-six goals and seventy-six assists for one hundred fifty-two points.

It was truly an unbelievable season for me. And when those 14,994 fans gave me a standing ovation I buried my face in my left arm on the bench and actually felt a little embarrassed. It was overwhelming.

I didn't realize it then, but genuine embarrassment would overwhelm me two weeks later.

We went into our opening-round playoff series against Montreal supremely confident. And why not? We had breezed to the Eastern Division championship while the Canadiens had finished third, twenty-four points behind us. We had rewritten the record book, setting eighteen team records and nineteen individual records. I had broken nine records. And the odds were 4½ to 1 in our favor. We couldn't lose.

The series opened at Boston Garden on Wednesday night, April 7. In our final practice on Tuesday I was seized by a strange feeling and discussed it with Fred Stanfield, my closest friend on the team.

"I don't know what's wrong with me, Fred," I said. "I feel weak and a little tired. How do you feel?"

"I don't feel right myself," Fred said. "But we've got to shake this off real fast."

We won the series opener, 3–1, but I must admit we were lucky. We played lousy. All of us, that is, except Gerry Cheevers. He was sensational in goal and kept us in the game. And Ken Dryden was just as great in the Montreal net. He was a rookie playing in his first playoff game, yet he didn't appear too nervous.

The second game was a nightmare. Looking back on it now it was probably the turning point of the series. We were skating rings around the Canadiens and leading, 5–1, late in the second period when Henri Richard stole the puck and went in alone to beat Ed Johnston. That triggered a chain-reaction of Montreal goals and before we knew it the score was tied.

Jean Beliveau scored twice in the first five minutes of the third period, then Jacques Lemaire tied the score at 5–5. Beliveau came back to set up a goal by John Ferguson, Frank Mahovlich scored into an empty net and the Canadiens won, 7–5.

To this day I don't know what the hell happened to us that night. I looked into the faces of some of our guys after the game and there was utter disbelief. They couldn't understand either how we could have blown a four-goal lead.

We traveled to Montreal for the next two games. I got my first playoff goal with only twenty-nine seconds gone in the third game, and I figured we were off and running again. But Dryden shut us out the rest of the way and the Canadiens won, 3–1.

Bobby Orr was brilliant in the fourth game. He became the first defenseman to score a three-goal hat trick in the playoffs and we won, 5–2. That tied the best-of-seven series at 2–2.

By this time most of our fans figured we would have swept right through the Canadiens and into the second round. But we knew we had a fight on our hands. Derek Sanderson probably said it best. "What you have to remember," he said, "is that the team we're playing is not the Motortown Rockets. These are the Montreal Canadiens. . . . These are good hockey players."

The Canadiens proved that to us again and again. After we won the fifth game at home, 7–3, they tied the series by whipping us, 8–3, at Montreal. Henri Richard and Pete Mahovlich each had two goals for them in that sixth game and Frank Mahovlich got two important assists.

So it all came down to the decisive seventh game at Boston Garden on Sunday afternoon, April 18. When Ken Hodge put us ahead with an unassisted goal in the first period the whole bench came alive. But we lost our momentum when the Canadiens went ahead, 2–1, on shots by Frank Mahovlich and Rejean Houle before the end of the opening period.

Now we were forced to play catch-up hockey and got a little sloppy. Jean-Claude Tremblay scored for Montreal in the second period after Jacques Lemaire stole the puck from Rick Smith. In the third period, Lemaire took the puck away from Orr and set up another goal by Frank Mahovlich.

That did it. The Canadiens skated off with a 4–2 victory and we skated back to our dressing room in a state of shock. The Boston Bruins had been eliminated from the playoffs — and it happened on our own rink where we had played like champions all season.

What happened? Many things, really. I didn't play as well as I had during the regular season, getting three goals in the seven games. I was frustrated many times by Dryden, who played one helluva series. But the thing that really hurt us was in letting the Canadiens take the play away from us after that awful defeat in the second game. They played their game and we didn't play ours. It was that simple.

As I sat in the dressing room after the game, I cried for the second time in my life. The first time I wept was after our juvenile team had won the All-Ontario championship back in Sault Ste. Marie and I had been named the Most Valuable Player. But those were tears of joy. These were tears of sorrow. I turned away from the other players so they couldn't see me and wept.

It would be up to Tony now to uphold our family's name in the playoffs.

> *The pressure Tony Esposito felt early in the season had continued to mount as the playoffs approached. Because of a broken arm suffered by the Black Hawks' backup goalie, Gerry Desjardins, Tony was forced to play in all but five of his team's games over the second half of the regular season. This "Iron Man" role taxed him physically and mentally and left him in an aggravated state for the start of the playoffs.*

I was aggravated all right — at myself and at the Hawks' management. I lost the Vezina Trophy, which goes to the league's top goalie, in the final week of the regular season. It wound up being shared by Ed Giacomin and Gilles Villemure of the Rangers. I also lost a five thousand dollar bonus the Hawks had promised me if I had finished the season with an average of 2.25 or better.

This was the real cause of my aggravation. Going into our final regular-season game against Toronto, my average was just a shade over 2.25. I wanted to sit out that game because I was exhausted, but Tommy Ivan told me if I didn't get my average down to 2.25 I could kiss the bonus goodbye. So I played and lost the game, 3–2, and the bonus.

I figured Ivan would give me the five thousand dollars anyway out of gratitude even though I finished at 2.27. Hell, I had played in fifty-seven of our seventy-eight games. In maybe half of those games I played with a banged up finger and never complained. And we did win the Western Division championship in a runaway, finishing twenty points ahead of second-place St. Louis.

But Ivan, like most general managers, stuck by the letter of my contract. "Sorry, Tony," he told me, "but I can't give you that bonus." He was sorry. I wonder if he considered how I felt.

So now we go into the opening round of the playoffs against Philadelphia and Desjardins is still out and I know we have no other experienced goalie to carry on if I get hurt. Talk about pressure!

It only took us the minimum four games to sweep the Flyers, although I must confess they played better than the record shows. And after that fourth game at Philadelphia I was dead on my skates. Thank God we had a week off waiting for the Rangers to eliminate the Maple Leafs. I needed that rest.

The semifinal series against the Rangers went seven games and was a humdinger. That's what Bobby Hull called it, and Bobby's been around for a while, you know. I figured this was a chance for me to get revenge on Giacomin and Villemure for beating me out of the Vezina. However, things didn't look too good for us when the Rangers won the first game on our home ice.

I had the Rangers shut out, 1–0, until Jean Ratelle beat me with less than four minutes left in regulation time. After only ninety-seven seconds of overtime, Bruce MacGregor passed the puck from the rear boards to Pete Stemkowski, who was in the faceoff circle to my left. Stemmer fired a quick wrist shot and it hit something and I couldn't see the puck. I prayed it would hit me, but it went in high to give the Rangers a 2–1 victory.

Giacomin suffered a cut hand in the opener and I didn't think he'd play in the second game. But he showed a lot of courage. He played the entire game, and I feel I was lucky to shut out the Rangers, 3–0. Vic Hadfield really bombed me in the third game, getting three goals, and we lost, 4–1.

We had two days off between the third and fourth games in New York, so Billy Reay took us back to Chicago. The coach didn't want us to stay around that jungle and maybe he was right. There are too many distractions for any athlete in New York.

After we beat the Rangers, 7–1, in the fourth game somebody asked Hadfield what happened to New York. Vic said, "We just fell on our duffs." He was so right. The Rangers landed on their duffs again when Bobby Hull's overtime goal gave us a 3–2 victory in the fifth game on our home ice.

The sixth game in New York had to be one of the greatest

playoff games in history. The score was tied 2–2 at the end of regulation time. It was still tied after the first overtime period. We should have won it in the second overtime when Giacomin got hit in the mask with a shot by Stan Mikita. While Eddie was down, Mikita and Bill White both missed shots at the empty net.

It was almost midnight when the third overtime period started. By this time everybody was dead. We were playing on guts alone. It all came down to a play that started when Ted Irvine shot from a tough angle to my right. If I had caught the puck, there would have been no rebound. But the puck hit my pads and bounced right out to Stemkowski, who was moving through the slot. He beat me before I even moved a muscle. The score came after one hundred and one minutes and twenty-nine seconds of play. Eighteen-and-a-half minutes more and it would have been like two games.

That tied the series at 3–3 and brought us back to Chicago for the final game. Our old pro, Bobby Hull, came through again. With the score tied at 2–2 in the third period, Lou Angotti beat Walt Tkaczuk to the draw in a faceoff in the New York end and passed to Bobby, who beat Giacomin with a wicked slap shot.

So now we found ourselves in the final round and our opponents would be the Canadiens, the same Canadiens who had blown Phil and the Bruins out of the playoffs. It was time for me to get a little more revenge.

I figured we really had those Flying Frenchmen grounded after winning the first two games at home. Jim Pappin's goal in the second overtime gave us the opener, 2–1, and we won the second game, 5–3, when Angotti banged in two goals in the third period.

Then I suffered an injury in the third game at Montreal that I hid from the reporters. It happened in the second period while the Canadiens were putting on one of their power plays. Jean Beliveau fired a shot and as I slid across the net to block it I pulled a muscle in my left leg.

The leg bothered me quite a bit for the rest of the game, which the Canadiens won, 4–2. When the reporters asked me about it later I had to lie to them. "Aw, it's nothing," I said. "I just got a cramp in my leg." I had to lie because I didn't want the Canadiens to know I was hurting.

The next day I could hardly walk, but I felt I had to play in

Frank Mahovlich of the Canadiens beats Tony in Stanley Cup series.

the fourth game because our backup goalie, Ken Brown, was too inexperienced. He had played less than a period of one game during the regular season. I was really suffering. Hell, I could barely move. I wasn't the only casualty. Stan Mikita had a badly-bruised foot and Pat Stapleton was weakened by a slashed cheekbone that required more than seventy stitches. So we lost the fourth game, 5–2, and now the Canadiens were flying again.

We split the next two games and by the time we skated out for the final game at Chicago Stadium my left leg was better. At least the pain had subsided. And when Dennis Hull and Danny O'Shea scored to give us a 2–0 lead I forgot all about the leg.

But we let the Canadiens off the hook. Jacques Lemaire and Henri Richard beat me late in the second period to tie the score. It was Lemaire's goal that really hurt. He fired from behind the blue line — maybe seventy feet out — and the puck dropped. I should have played it off the body. Instead, I tried to catch it and missed.

We went into our locker room after the second period knowing this was it. It had come down to the final twenty minutes — the whole season, the whole ball of wax. We sat there quietly, nobody saying anything.

Phil was in the TV booth in the Stadium, serving as an analyst for the game which was being televised nationally. I didn't find out until later that when Lemaire scored, Phil remarked, "Well, Tony blew that one." He was right, too. I had blown it.

I was really uptight when we skated out for the final period. With less than three minutes gone, Richard broke in on me from left wing after getting by Keith Magnuson. I couldn't commit myself by coming out, so I tried to stay with him. Then, as Henri cut in front of me, he shot it back and caught a corner of the net.

That broke the tie and it broke my heart. Our guys tried hard to get it back, but Ken Dryden, who had played so well in goal for the Canadiens throughout the entire playoffs, wouldn't budge. The funny thing is we had plenty of time after Richard's second goal to get back in the game, but it seemed like it took only two minutes to play the entire period. It went that fast.

So the Canadiens were the Stanley Cup champions — again. They had beaten Phil and they had beaten me.

CHAPTER XX

OUR GANG

*What is Bobby Hull really like? Does he save
that marvelous smile for the fans and turn it off
behind the closed doors of the locker room? And
how about Bobby Orr? How does he act off the ice?
Here the Espositos discuss the superstars and the
not-so-super players on their respective teams. Phil,
as the oldest, was given the privilege of leading off.*

I suppose the easiest way to handle this is to run down the
Boston roster in numerical order. So here goes:

Ed Johnston (No. 1): We call him "E.J." He is the most astute
student of the game on our team. He has an analytical mind and
should make a great coach some day. He has always been helpful
to me. If I'm having trouble scoring against a certain goalie he's
the guy I go to. Before a game, I'll ask him for his opinion of the
opposing goalie, how I should shoot against him, should I keep my
shot high or low. Ed is one of the league's most underrated goalies.
When the Bruins had those bad teams he stuck it out and took a
lot of abuse. He's improved tremendously in the past couple of
years. I like to bug him about his age — he's thirty-six — but he
accepts the kidding good-naturedly. I've never met a goalie who
wasn't a good beer drinker and Ed is no exception.

Bobby Orr (No. 4): His on-the-ice exploits are listed in the
record books. I would add only one thought here: In every game
he shows me something different. I have always been awed by
the things Gordie Howe and Bobby Hull could do with the puck.
Bobby Orr does them better. Off the ice, Orr is a pretty comical
guy. He has a dry sense of humor and is a practical joker. I've been

187

his victim on occasions. Once, after a game in Pittsburgh, I pulled on my socks and yanked them all the way up to my thighs. While the guys howled, I discovered holes had been cut out of the bottom of each sock. I looked across the room at Bobby and said, "I'll bet you're responsible for this." He gave me that innocent grin and said, "Not me, Phil." What a liar. Bobby is a fun guy and he keeps us loose in the dressing room. There was a time when he didn't mix too much with the other guys. But now he's one of the gang and he likes parties.

Teddy Green (No. 6): He is the man I thought I'd have trouble with when I was traded to the Bruins. While I was with Chicago I considered him tough and mean. I roomed with him during my first year in Boston. He was a tough guy to get to know. He was a little self-centered then. He wanted to be left alone and wouldn't take any crap from anybody. But now I can't say enough about the guy. He's the most courageous player I know. I never could have made the comeback he did. Teddy did it and now he's a changed man. He is always smiling and joking. He has learned to take a little kidding and can dish it out, too. I think he came to realize what type of friends he had on the team after his near-fatal accident and this meant a lot to him.

Phil Esposito (No. 7): Let's skip him. He gets too much publicity anyway.

Ken Hodge (No. 8): Kenny and I have known each other for more than eight years. He would do anything for me, I'm sure of it. But I must be perfectly frank about Kenny. Until the past year he was still a kid growing up. When we were with Chicago and he was just breaking in, he used to get in trouble with some of the guys. He would make insulting statements that were both silly and stupid. I know he didn't mean them as insults, but some players resented them. This continued for a while when we were traded to Boston. He had trouble with Harry Sinden. It was a sort of personality conflict. Some guys just don't get along with their coach. Kenny and Harry simply didn't hit it off. All this changed when Tom Johnson succeeded Sinden. Kenny finally matured and had a great season. I really like the guy now. He works his butt off for me on the ice and he's developed into one helluva hockey player.

John Bucyk (No. 9): He is one of the truly great team captains in the game. As far as the players are concerned he's a far better captain than Pierre Pilote was during our days in Chicago. John is known as "Chief" to most people but we call him "Mr. Arrangement." If there is a party to be arranged, John arranges it. If you need something special, Johnny will get it. He takes care of everything. And on the ice he is simply amazing. Imagine scoring more than fifty goals in your sixteenth year in the league. He's really Johnny-on-the-spot.

Rick Smith (No. 10): I call him "Harpo" because of his mop of hair. He's considered our fifth defenseman, but he could play regularly on any other team and probably be an All-Star. It's just unfortunate he's with the Bruins in that respect. Mark my words, Rick has the stuff to develop into a premier defenseman. He's also extremely intelligent. He has attended Queens University in Kingston and wants to be a dentist. But he's not a high-brow type. I enjoy joking around with him and Gerry Cheevers.

Wayne Cashman (No. 12): What a fighter this guy is. He is absolutely fearless. His left hook is the best in the league. He is the type of kid who loses his confidence very easily and requires an occasional pat on the back. Whenever I can do anything to help him I do it willingly because I love him like a brother.

Ace Bailey (No. 14): Like Rick Smith, he could play regularly on any other team in the league. He just hasn't had the chance. But he's young and I feel is a potential star. The thing I like about Ace is that he's a great team man. Even when he isn't playing, his spirit is good. In the dressing room, he keeps everybody in stitches. He's always jovial and I feel this is important.

Derek Sanderson (No. 16): He thinks most of the guys on the team dislike him. He's wrong. He says I'm his best friend and I hope so. I think some of his ideas are strange, but I think this is just a put-on to get publicity. When he says he doesn't believe in God, this upsets me and I walk away from him. Yet he will discuss things with me that he would never discuss with anybody else on the team. He's not as hard as he makes himself out to be. Actually, he's a soft-hearted individual and a romantic at heart. I really dig Derek. As a player he still doesn't realize the potential he has. When he does, he'll be a real star.

Fred Stanfield (No. 17): He's the quiet man on the team. We've been close friends for more than ten years. We're in business together and we take vacation trips together with our families. He's my best friend on the club, no doubt about it. I'd trust him with my life. The unfortunate thing about Fred is that he's in the same boat I was in at Chicago when I played behind Stan Mikita. As a center, he plays second banana to me. But he never bugs anybody about it. He goes out and does his job in every stinking game and gets his twenty to twenty-five goals a season.

Eddie Westfall (No. 18): Although we have been teammates for four years, I don't know too much about Eddie. He's a loner who goes off by himself on the road. He is a great team man, though. If there's a job to be done anywhere, Eddie will step in and do it. Although normally used at right wing, he has filled in as a defenseman and done well. He and Derek are our best penalty-killers. He's a pipe-smoker, intelligent and sort of a leveling influence on some of the kooks on the club.

John McKenzie (No. 19): A very funny man. We bug each other silly in the dressing room. Most people know he's a cowboy who used to work the rodeo circuit as a calf-roper, but there's another side to old Pie. He is deathly afraid of horror movies. I check the TV listings in the paper and tell him this is the night that Dracula is on the late show and give him that spooky bit. On the ice he is like Bucyk — a player who the older he gets the better he gets.

Dallas Smith (No. 20): He's a farm boy from Manitoba, a very quiet individual. The only time he ever shows any real emotion is when he tells you about his life on the farm. Still, he can be very funny when he's had a few drinks, though he's not a boozer by any means. To me he was one of the most underrated defensemen in the league for a long time and it's nice to see him finally getting the recognition he deserves.

Don Marcotte (No. 21): He has personality-plus although he doesn't always give people that impression because he's not flamboyant. An easy guy to get along with. We travel together a lot. He didn't play too much under Sinden, but has seen more action under Johnson. A tough body-checker. When he hits you it hurts.

Mike Walton (No. 25): His nickname is "Shaky." He had his troubles in Toronto but seemed to fit right in with our crew. Maybe that's because we have so many flakey players. In the short time he's been with us, Mike has shown he is friendly and a good worker. He seems to be a nice guy.

Don Awrey (No. 26): Green's partner on defense. He's often overlooked by the public and the press, but he does a helluva job. He looks and acts mean on the ice, but he's actually an even-tempered man. Very quiet in the dressing room. Don and I get along real well. We pal around together quite a bit. I consider him a close friend.

Reg Leach (No. 27): Keep your eye on this kid. You're going to hear a lot from him in the next couple of seasons. He's part Indian and all player. He was our first pick in the 1970 amateur draft and made the big jump to Boston last season. The only thing that could hurt him now would be for somebody to lead him astray, but I think Reg is too smart to let that happen.

Gerry Cheevers (No. 30): Cheesy is the comedian on the Bruins. He's an unbelievably funny guy. Oddly, he gets down on himself if he loses or is victimized by a bad call, but it doesn't take long for him to shake the blues. Then he's back cracking jokes with the rest of us. He loves horses, lives and breathes the sport. He claims if there is such a thing as reincarnation he would like to return as a horse. And he means it!

So much for the Bruins' players. Regarding our coach, Tom Johnson, I feel he was very fortunate in his first (1970-71) season. He inherited a great club from Harry Sinden. We won a lot of games for Tom — no other team ever won more. As a rookie coach, he could have come in and screwed things up but he didn't. But you can't really tell what kind of a coach he is after only one season. I feel more comfortable with Tom, though, than I did with Sinden.

Sometimes I don't agree with Johnson's strategy on matchups. I feel you can outcoach a guy in your own rink because of that option you have of making the last move. Sinden was great at that. Suppose we were playing Montreal. Harry used to match me against Jean Beliveau. When Beliveau took the ice, I took the ice. When he came off, I came off.

With Johnson that has all changed. He doesn't concern himself with matchups. Tom will say, "Just go out there and play. We don't have to worry about anybody." Maybe he's right. Still, I feel if you can get the jump on the other guy you may as well take it.

One more thing about Tom Johnson: He's from the old school and demands respect. He gets ticked off at guys who answer him back. I don't blame him. If I was coach I'd be the same way. Let 'em know who's boss.

He proved who was boss at practice one day last season. One of our guys showed up a little hung over. He had been out all night. Tom skated his butt off in practice. But the longer the guy stayed on the ice the better he played. Finally some of the vets went to Johnson and said, "C'mon, Tom, get that guy off the ice. He's killing us out there." Tom still laughs whenever he's reminded of that incident.

Who was the guy he tried to discipline? I wouldn't reveal that for a million dollars.

When Tom tires of coaching I feel he'll make a good general manager. He has a great background. But I wouldn't want to see him get that job as long as Milt Schmidt is still around. I like Milt and feel he is an immensely capable GM. Why shouldn't I feel that way? Milt is the guy who rescued me from the Chicago dung heap.

Regarding other players in the league, I respect most of them. Howe, the Hulls and Ratelle are super guys. And I really dug Beliveau. Hockey is a tough enough sport to play without having disrespect for anyone. Of course, there are a couple in the league who are complete idiots. But I don't want to mention any names and provide them with additional ammunition.

The best referee? Man, that's a hard one. I know the referees are yelled at quite a bit and take a lot of abuse. But, my God, you can't even talk to these guys. I don't yell very often at them, but sometimes when I do get so incensed I have to shout to be heard. If only they would listen to you. Instead, they give you the deaf ear and that tees me off. The worst referee is Ron Wicks, and that's as far as I want to go on that subject.

The New York fans get my vote as the worst in hockey. Right behind them are the Chicago fans. I suppose the fans are good as long as you're winning. In Boston, during those years when the Bruins were losing, the people still showed up. Of course, they booed a lot. Hell, they boo now when we lose a game. And I don't mind that. It's the name-calling and the missile-throwing that's bad. I can recall one game in New York when a padlock was thrown on the ice. Eggs and tomatoes are bad enough, but a padlock! Whew. We've also had rocks thrown at our player bus in New York. We can't do anything to retaliate or we'd be sued. The league should do something to curb that nonsense. And it had better act soon before somebody is seriously injured.

Okay, Tony, what are your Black Hawk team-mates really like, off and on the ice?

When you think of the Black Hawks you think first of Bobby Hull. I know I always do. There is nothing phony about Bobby, his smile or his attitude toward people in general.

You hear stories about Bobby holding up the team bus in New York or Detroit or Los Angeles while he obliges all the kids who want his autograph. It's true. I've never seen him turn his back on any kid. He considers it an obligation or as he likes to say, "It's part of the job" of being a superstar.

And Bobby Hull is a superstar. He still shoots the puck harder than anybody. And in the past couple of years he's become more of a playmaker. I've seen times when he's had good chances to score and passed off to Chico Maki or Bryan Campbell or Pit Martin because he felt they were in a better position to go for an open corner.

I consider this real teamwork. Bobby likes to score goals and he hasn't lost his touch there. He was right up among the scoring leaders in 1970-71. But he doesn't worry as much about goals as he does about winning the game — and that's no bull.

Bobby also has a superb personality. He walks into our dressing room and gives everybody a warm greeting. It always makes me feel good just to see that guy getting into his uniform. He's friendly with everybody and he's been great to me from the time I joined the club as a rookie.

After many games, I'm wound up for two or three hours. Really uptight. So I'll go out with the guys for a few beers. If Bobby is there, he helps us all relax. He'll tell us about his cattle or his early days in the league and soon we've forgotten all about that night's game. And when it's Bobby's turn to buy a round he always makes sure he doesn't miss anybody.

Dennis Hull has many of his brother's great qualities. Dennis has never had it easy in Chicago. The fans have made life miserable for him. When they boo him he worries because he wants to perform as well as Bobby and he wants the fans to like him.

I was happy about the great year Dennis had in 1970-71 because the Chicago Stadium crowd finally started to appreciate him. I feel the fans would appreciate him more if they could get to know him off the ice because he's very jovial and a likeable guy.

Jim Pappin has gone through a lot of misery with the Chicago fans, too. And he hasn't been able to handle it as well as Dennis because Jim is a wee bit temperamental. He gets aggravated quicker and then he becomes moody and sulks a lot and this hurts the team.

The only time I get disillusioned about playing in Chicago is when the fans get on a player's back and won't get off. I think this is unwarranted, especially in the case of Pappin and, before him, Dennis Hull. These men are professionals. Both of them have done good work over the years. They've helped the team, believe me. But when the fans get on them, you'd be surprised how they react. It really gets on their nerves and affects their play.

I hate it when they boo me. They do it sometimes and even though I might be having a bad night and figure I deserve it, it still gets under my skin. The booing affects your whole life, even off the ice. You take it out on your wife. You get aggravated with her because you're angry at the fans. It's silly, but it happens.

Another Chicago player who has lost patience with the fans on occasions is Stan Mikita. When the Hawks failed to make the playoffs in 1969, the fans got on Stan pretty good. They figured he was having a bad year when all he did was score thirty goals and ninety-seven points. How about that?

Mikita is a fantastic centerman. I think Phil is the best at that position, naturally, but Stan is right behind him. He's another good team man. He sets up his wingers like nobody else in hockey. He carries the puck well. And he has a lot of courage.

Stan had trouble with his back in 1970-71, but few people knew about it. He played many games when I'm sure he was in great pain. You have to admire a guy like that. He knew he wasn't one hundred per cent, yet he went out there and did his best.

They say a goalie is only as good as the defensemen in front of him. I'll buy that. Our four regular defensemen —Pat Stapleton, Bill White, Keith Magnuson and Doug Jarrett — gave me terrific protection. Without them, we never would have reached the final of the 1971 Stanley Cup playoffs.

Stapleton has to be the most underrated defenseman in the league. He's not as good as Bobby Orr. Who is? But I'd put him right behind Orr. Here's what I think of Pat Stapleton: I'd sooner have him in front of me than any defenseman I've ever played with and, remember, I played behind some good ones at Montreal.

Pat isn't too big. He's about five-foot-eight and weighs one hundred eighty-five pounds. He can't bodycheck guys all over the ice, but what he lacks in brawn he makes up in brains and great anticipation. He and White make a great pair on defense. We call them "Mutt and Jeff." Bill is a big guy, standing six-foot-two and weighing close to two hundred pounds. It's his job to cover up for Stapleton when Pat lugs the puck out of our end and starts up ice. White does his job well. And he can shoot, too. He has a dangerous shot from the point.

Magnuson is the most colorful of the Hawks' defensemen with his flaming red hair and his hell-for-leather style of skating. I like Keith. When he first joined the Hawks he used to draw some bad penalties. But I've never gotten angry with him because I know when he's out there he's always giving one hundred per cent. He's developed a reputation as a fighter and I do know he has taken lessons in karate. In this respect, Keith might be a little overrated. He's not a great fighter. He's just a good, honest, tough player.

Jarrett, I feel, could use some of Magnuson's aggressiveness. Doug is one of the best body-checkers in the league, but he won't fight anybody. His main problem is he's such an easy-going guy. You can't aggravate him. I've tried and failed. He claims he doesn't want to hurt anybody and, in a way, I don't blame him. Doug works hard, though. He wouldn't have lasted this long in Chicago if he didn't, believe me.

Bryan Campbell and Gerry Pinder, two of our younger forwards, got messed up a little bit in the 1970-71 season. Campbell may be his own worst enemy. If he doesn't have a good game, he broods a lot. I'm not a psychiatrist, but I've tried to help Bryan. "Forget that last game," I'll say, "and try harder the next time. If you start second-guessing yourself, you're going to make more mistakes." Bryan will look at me and say, "Okay, Tony, I'll try." And he does try. But then he starts brooding again, and this hurts him and his play.

Pinder got into trouble with management during the 1971 playoffs. He was upset because he hadn't been playing regularly, mouthed off to the press and then quit the club. He rejoined the team later after apologizing for his remarks. His problem all stemmed back to early in the season when he missed four or five good opportunities to score. He got discouraged, just like Campbell, and soon found himself sitting on the bench.

I'm certain, though, that Pinder and Campbell can make it in the National Hockey League. Once they regain their confidence, they're going to score a lot of goals.

The Hawks, like most clubs, have a couple of players who lean on their sticks and dog it once in a while. There is no point in identifying them now. But Billy Reay knows who they are and if they're not with the club by the time this book is published, you'll know why they were traded.

INDEX

197